D0203733

GEORGIA'S INDIAN HERITAGE:

The Prehistoric Peoples and Historic Tribes

of Georgia

By Max E. White, Ph.D.

Library of Congress Catalog Number
88-50447

WH Wolfe Associates
P.O. Box 972
Roswell, Georgia 30077

The initial phase of research for
this book was funded by a Clemson
University Provost Award.

ACKNOWLEDGEMENTS

I wish to acknowledge the assistance of the following individuals in making the writing of this book possible: Dr. and Mrs. Kent Schneider, Mr. Robert Palmer, Dr. David J. Hally, Mr. Thomas Beutell, Mr. Alan Marsh, Mr. Billy Townsend, my parents, Mr. and Mrs. Ralph E. White, and (especially) my wife, Jeanne.

FOREWORD

The idea to write this book was the culmination of a lifelong interest in history, archaeology, and other cultures, particularly American Indians. I grew up in Banks County, Georgia, which lies within the former Cherokee Nation and is steeped in Indian lore. As a youngster, I found "arrowheads" and bits of pottery in our cotton- and cornfields. My great-grandparents could remember when small bands of Cherokees lived along the Hudson River, some fifty years after the Removal. My fascination with Indians persisted through high school, and in college, I found that the field of anthropology embodied my interests. I was awarded the A.B. degree in anthropology by the University of Georgia in 1968, and the M.A. degree in 1970. After teaching at Western Carolina University, I continued graduate studies at Indiana University, Bloomington, Indiana, where I was awarded the Ph.D. degree in anthropology in 1980. It is my most sincere wish that all who read these pages may come to a greater appreciation of Georgia's first people and their contributions to our common heritage.

Max E. White
March 1, 1988

Chapter I

INTRODUCTION

*A*merican Indians! Archaeology! These are subjects which capture the interest of almost everyone. Yet, our knowledge of these subjects is often limited and clouded by misconceptions and myths. One cannot long remain in Georgia without being aware of the numerous reminders of the peoples who lived here before the Europeans came. Counties, cities, rivers, and mountains bear names derived from the Creek, Cherokee, and other Indian languages. Who were these people who lived in what is now Georgia when the Spaniards and English arrived? How did they dress? How did they make a living? What were their houses and settlements like? How long had they been here?

These are questions often asked, and most can be answered readily enough, thanks to the work of archaeologists. But the last question is more involved. The tribes encountered by the Europeans had been in what is now Georgia for probably only a few hundred years. There is evidence, however, that people lived here for thousands of years. Who were these early Indians, and what was their life like? The information in the following pages will attempt to answer these and other questions about Georgia's original inhabitants.

It is through the findings of archaeologists, anthropologists, and ethnohistorians that we may come to appreciate Georgia's Indian heritage and what it means to us today. The picture is by no means complete, however, as archaeologists are limited by the types of evidence which survive. Unlike arid parts of our country, the climate and soils of the Southeast have not allowed preservation of many archaeological clues. Except in rare instances, perishable artifacts, such as wood, fiber, hair, sinew, and basketry, are gone. Thus, archaeologists working in the eastern part of the continent are largely restricted to interpreting past life-ways through such lasting evidence as stone, bone, or ceramic materials. It is good to keep in mind that only a portion of the artifacts used by a group will remain. Those that do remain, when properly excavated, can tell us a great deal about life in the past. But before we explore this fascinating realm of archaeological discovery, let us turn to a brief overview of archaeology in Georgia.

The history of archaeology in Georgia began with the writings of early travelers (scientists, military and government officials, et al.) through the state. One of the first explorers was the botanist, William Bartram. Bartram was one of those rare individuals who combined extensive scientific knowledge with a talent for getting along with

1

William Bartram, the botanist who described Indian life in Georgia in the mid-1700's. *(Courtesy Independence National Historical Park Collection)* **Photo No. 1**

people wherever he went. A keen observer, he noted several locations in Georgia where prehistoric remains could be seen. His first trip to the state began in April, 1773, when he set out from Charleston, S.C., traveling to Augusta. Leaving Augusta, he accompanied a surveying team to the settlement of Wrightsborough, and it was near there, on the Little River, where he discovered:

"many very magnificent monuments of the power and industry of the ancient inhabitants of these lands . . . . I observed a stupendous conical pyramid, or

2

artificial mount of earth, vast tetragon terraces, and a large sunken area, of a cubicle form, encompassed with banks of earth; and certain traces of a larger Indian town, the work of a powerful nation, whose period of grandeur perhaps long preceded the discovery of this continent."

(Bartram 1955:56-7).

Bartram also gives the following description of the Ocmulgee site at Macon:

"On the heights of these low grounds are yet visible monuments, or traces, of an ancient town, such as artificial mounts or terraces, squares and banks, encircling considerable areas."

(Bartram 1955:68).

He adds that the local Creek Indians claimed this as the site of their first settlement upon arrival from the west.

In April of 1776, Bartram again visited Georgia, this time embarking for the Cherokee country from Augusta. On this trip, he visited a site near the confluence of the Broad and Savannah Rivers. He writes:

"These wonderful labours of the ancients stand in a level plain, very near the bank of the river . . . . They consist of conical mounts of earth and four square terraces. The great mount is in the form of a cone, about forty or fifty feet high, and the circumference of its base two or three hundred yards . . . . the top or apex is flat: a spiral path or track leading from the ground up to the top is visible . . . . there appear four niches, excavated out of the sides of this hill, at different heights from the base, fronting the four cardinal points; these niches or sentry boxes are entered into from the winding path, and seem to have been meant for resting places or look-outs."

(Bartram 1955:265-6).

Bartram adds that this entire site, including the mound just described, was even then under cultivation.

Following early descriptions like those of Bartram, only a few other writings are relevant to Georgia archaeology until late in the nineteenth century. These are found in the form of letters written to the Smithsonian Institution by various interested individuals and published as part of the Smithsonian Annual Reports. The Annual Report for 1872 contains one such letter, written by M.F. Stephenson, in which the Etowah site is described, as well as aboriginal fortifications on Stone Mountain, Yonah Mountain, and on a small hill near the Nacoochee site (Stephenson 1873:421-2).

The major publication pertaining to Georgia archaeology during the early period is *Antiquities of the Southern Indians, Particularly the Georgia Tribes,* published by C.C. Jones in 1873. Of this volume, Waring writes that it "was intelligently planned and clearly written" (Waring in Williams 1965:289). The book can be divided into three parts: (1) a discussion of aboriginal tribal customs based on the accounts of early explorers; (2) descriptions and maps of mound groups in Georgia; and (3) a discussion of the types of artifacts found in the state (see Waring *ibid.*). Despite some mistakes, and despite his primitive techniques of excavation, Jones was ahead of his time in concluding that the mound-builders were not a race "distinct from and superior in art, government, and religion, to the Southern Indians of the fifteenth and sixteenth centuries" (Waring *op. cit.*:290).

This was in fact, the conclusion reached by the renowned archaeologist, Cyrus Thomas, who headed up mound explorations by the Bureau of American Ethnology beginning in 1882. Using what are now regarded as unacceptable archaeological techniques, Thomas and his assistants dug trenches or pits into more than 2,000 mounds scattered over the eastern United States. In 1883 and 1884, Thomas' assistants, Cochran, Middleton, and Rogan, worked in Georgia. John P. Rogan dug at the Etowah site and at other mound sites in White, Rabun, Habersham, McIntosh, and Forsyth Counties. In Elbert County, he dug into the mounds described about a hundred years earlier by Bartram. Rogan worked at other sites in Bartow County, but his investigations at the Etowah site were of primary significance. In brief, Mound C was trenched by his team, and burials containing copper plates were encountered. The material proved so interesting that William Henry Holmes, another well-known archaeologist of the time, visited Etowah and made the first accurate drawings of the mounds and other features of this important site.

It was during this same period that Edward Palmer, also of the Bureau of American Ethnology, began investigations at the Kolomoki site near Blakely, Early County. His work consisted of digging pits and/or trenches into several mounds on this large site, but despite all his work, he found nothing worth cataloging and not a single burial (Waring *op. cit.*:292).

In Waring's estimation (*op. cit.*:293), the most competent archaeological work of the period was that conducted by Henry L. Reynolds at the Hollywood Mounds, located on the Savannah River a few miles below Augusta. He completely excavated the smaller of the two mounds, which was found to have been built in three stages. In the earliest mound, Reynolds found artifacts now known to be associated with the "Southern Cult," including copper plates, effigy vessels, painted or engraved pottery, and pipes of a distinctive type. The second mound stage contained more burials, but none of the elaborate cult artifacts. Ceramics of this second stage are recognized as being transitional between the Savannah II and Irene periods (see Chapter VI). The final mound stage contained no burials, and historic artifacts found in this level are now believed to have been associated with a nineteenth century house which stood on the mound (Waring *op. cit.*:293).

In 1896, the renowned archaeologist, Clarence B. Moore, investigated mounds along the Georgia coast and wrote up his findings the following year (Moore 1897). However, the excavations which are called the "first piece of professional archaeology in Georgia" by Waring (*op. cit.*:294) took place at the Nacoochee Mound in White County. The mound is now known to date from the late prehistoric period and most of the artifacts found during its excavation are in the Museum of the American Indian, Heye Foundation, New York City. More mound investigations were undertaken in 1927-28 when Warren K. Moorehead arrived at the Etowah site and began excavating in Mound C (see Chapter VI). A movement away from temple and burial mound exploration was heralded by excavations at Stallings Island in the Savannah River near Augusta (Claflin 1931), and archaeology in Georgia really got under way during the Roosevelt era when it was used as a means of providing much-needed jobs. It was during this time that A.R. Kelly came to supervise the excavations at Macon.

Kelly, a native Texan, was a Harvard graduate with training in physical anthropology and archaeology. His casual approach, as well as his education, won him the

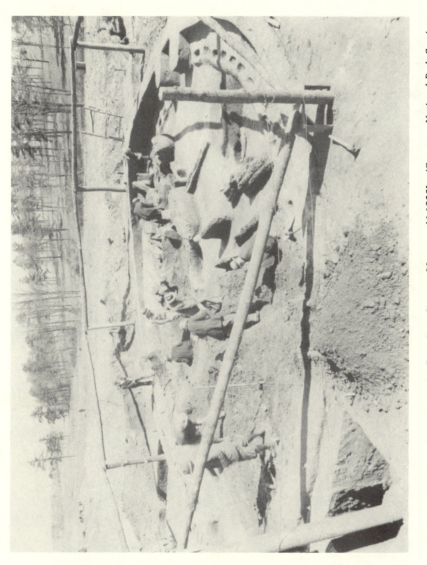

Excavation of the earth lodge at the Ocmulgee site near Macon, mid-1930's. *(Courtesy National Park Service, Ocmulgee National Monument)* Photo No. 2

respect of the workers and facilitated his efforts at locating sites in the Macon area and throughout the state. He was in charge of the excavations at the Ocmulgee site, where several of the most renowned archaeologists in the United States worked at the beginning of their careers. Kelly went on to take a position on the faculty at the University of Georgia, where he remained until retirement in 1968. During his career, he became the "grand old man" of Georgia archaeology and was known affectionately as "Doc" to farmers and students alike throughout the state.

Dr. A.R. Kelly, the foremost figure in Georgia archaeology for more than thirty years. *(Courtesy Department of Anthropology, University of Georgia)* **Photo No. 3**

Growing interest in the archaeology of Georgia is exemplified by the organization of the Society for Georgia Archaeology in the fall of 1933. The society's first meeting was held at Macon and included two days of field trips to the excavations in progress on the Macon Plateau, Brown's Mount, and the Lamar site (Smith 1939:15). The society began publication of *Early Georgia* in 1950, but the society and the journal ceased to exist a few years later. Both were reconstituted, however, in the 1970's, and the society now holds regular meetings and has regional chapters in several parts of the state.

One of the archaeologists who participated in excavations sponsored by the W.P.A. in Georgia, and one who would come to play a primary role in Georgia archaeology, was Joseph R. Caldwell. Married to the daughter of A.R. Kelly, Caldwell worked for the Smithsonian Institution and the Illinois State Museum prior to returning to Georgia in 1967 as a faculty member at the University. He was director of the Laboratory of Archaeology and conducted surveys and excavations throughout the state until his untimely death in 1973. Like Kelly, Caldwell was easy-going and personable, traits which were admired by all who came to know him (see Schneider and Crusoe 1976).

Dr. Joseph R. Caldwell and the author, St. Catherines Island, 1969. Photo No. 4

Other archaeologists who have conducted research in Georgia in recent years include Milanich (University of Florida), Thomas (American Museum of Natural History), Dickens (formerly at Georgia State University), and Hally (University of Georgia). In addition, numerous personnel affiliated with several business enterprises have engaged in surveys and excavations in Georgia in recent years. This latter has been in connection with legislation requiring environmental impact statements for archaeological resources in areas targeted for construction, if government funding is involved. Thus it is that "business archaeology" is now being carried out throughout the state. In addition to archaeologists affiliated with colleges and universities, and those of the business world, some archaeologists are employed by State or Federal agencies. The Department of Transportation and the U.S. Forest Service are examples of agencies where archaeologists are now important personnel.

Archaeology has provided us with virtually all that we know about how people lived in Georgia before the coming of the Europeans. Admittedly, large areas of the state have not received the attention they deserve from archaeologists, and for this reason many counties and sites are not mentioned in the following pages. It is hoped that in the future, each county will receive the attention of archaeologists working through the University System to increase our knowledge of the state's prehistory. Our archaeological resources are as important as any of our other cultural resources and must be conserved accordingly. It is only in this way that future generations can appreciate the cultural heritage of all Georgians, particularly for the thousands of years before history began.

REFERENCES: CHAPTER I

Bartram, William, *Travels of William Bartram*, Ed. by Mark Van Doren, Dover Publications, New 1955 York.

Claflin, W.H., Jr., "The Stallings Island Mound, Columbia County, Georgia," *Papers of the Peabody* 1931 *Museum of American Archaeology, and Ethnology, No. 14.*

Jones, Charles C., *Antiquities of the Southern Indians, Particularly of the Georgia Tribes*, D. Apple- 1873 ton and Co., New York.

Moore, Clarence B., "Certain Aboriginal Mounds of the Georgia Coast," *Academy of Natural* 1897 *Sciences of Philadelphia, Journal*, Vol. 2.

Schneider, Kent A., and Donald L. Crusoe, "Joseph Ralston Caldwell, 1916-1973," *American* 1976 *Antiquity*, Vol. 41, No. 3, pp. 303-307.

Smith, Richard W., "A History of the Society for Georgia Archaeology," *Proceedings of the So-* 1939 *ciety for Georgia Archaeology*, Vol. 2, No. 2, pp. 13-17.

Stephenson, M.F., "Mounds in Bartow County, Near Cartersville, Georgia," in *Annual Report of* 1873 *the Smithsonian Institution, 1872*, Government Printing Office, Washington, pp. 421-2.

Waring, Antonio J., Jr., "A History of Georgia Archaeology to World War II," in *The Waring* 1965 *Papers: The Southern Cult, and Other Archaeological Essays*, Ed. by Stephen Williams, University of Georgia Press, Athens, pp. 288-299.

Chapter II

ENVIRONMENT

*T*he area of what is now Georgia is quite diverse in its geology, geography, and plant and animal life. Unlike some other areas of the country, Georgia's natural environment was and is a rich one and would have been ideal for a population of hunter-gatherers. Being the largest state east of the Mississippi, it includes a variety of natural settings (see Wharton 1978) where a wide range of species of plants and animals is found. Always, the relationship between environment and culture is an intimate one and peoples living in what is now Georgia learned to exploit the area's various resources in a variety of ways. These native peoples all practiced hunting, fishing, and gathering, either exclusively or in part, and thus a brief description of the geographical areas (physiographic provinces), geology, and plant and animal life is essential to gaining a more complete understanding of the life of Georgia's prehistoric inhabitants.

Almost all of Georgia was forest-covered when the Europeans first appeared on the scene. There is, and was, a variety of forest types in the state, each with its own distinctive makeup of tree species, shrubs, herbs, birds, and animals. Some idea of the complexity of these natural communities can be gained from Wharton's (*op. cit.*) monumental work. Types of trees and other plants are seen to vary according to soil type, the type of underlying bedrock, presence or absence of water, and many other local or regional factors, not to mention climate. Different life forms are found in the various microenvironments in the same forest, i.e., swampy lowlands, uplands, coves, ravines, sinks, north-facing hillsides, rivers and riverbottoms, etc. This complexity and diversity of life was to some extent known to, and exploited by Georgia's prehistoric inhabitants. There follows a brief description of each of the five geographic regions in the state, along with a discussion of some of the natural resources of each area. Many of these resources were of economic importance to native peoples.

Geographic Provinces

Appalachian (Cumberland) Plateau Province

In extreme northwest Georgia, Dade County and parts of Walker and Chattooga Counties are included in the Appalachian, or Cumberland, Plateau province (see Map 1). This area forms the western boundary of the Great Valley and is typified by an undulating or hilly surface through which streams have cut rather steep-sided valleys. The boundary between this province and the Great Valley is marked by steep cliffs which

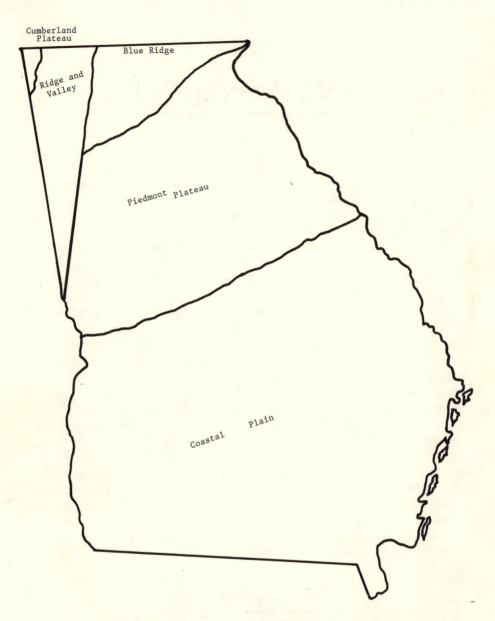

The Geographic Provinces of Georgia. Map No. 1.

can be seen along the sides of Lookout, Sand, and Pigeon Mountains (Fenneman 1938: 334-38). These mountains are quite flat on top and are unlike any other topographic features in Georgia (see Wharton *op. cit.*:108). This area is underlain by limestone and other sedimentary rocks, and except for the valleys, has rather thin, poor soil (Campbell in La Forge et al. 1925:155). The northern part of this region in Georgia is drained by streams flowing into the Tennessee River, while streams in the southern part of the area empty into the Coosa River (Campbell *op. cit.*).

10

The top and slopes of the Appalachian Plateau in Georgia are covered in an oak-hickory forest where chestnut oak (*Quercus montana*), white oak (*Q. alba*), post oak (*Q. stellata*), blackjack oak (*Q. marilandica*), northern red oak (*Q. borealis*), Southern red oak (*Q. falcata*), and yellow poplar (*Liriodendron tulipifera*) predominate. Formerly, chestnut (*Castanea dentata*) also grew here.

Ridge and Valley Province

This portion of northwest Georgia (see Map 1) is a part of the Great Valley, a feature which includes the ridges and valleys stretching northeastward across east Tennessee and on up the western boundary of the Appalachian Mountains. This area in Georgia is underlain by sedimentary rocks. Lying west of the Blue Ridge province, its eastern boundary largely follows the geologic contacts between the older rocks of the Blue Ridge and the younger rocks of the Great Valley. This boundary is reflected in the noticeably different topography, the parallel ridges and valleys on the west contrasting sharply with the mountainous terrain of the Blue Ridge to the east (Thornbury 1965; Miller 1974). It is in this province that deposits of chert, used by prehistoric peoples for tool manufacture, are most numerous. Chert sources occur sporadically in the southeastern portion of the province, and increase in abundance in the northwestern part (Goad 1979:18). Of the several types found here, Copper Ridge Dolomite chert and Fort Payne chert appear to have been the types most heavily utilized by native peoples (Goad *op. cit.*).

The forest of the Ridge and Valley Province is the oak-hickory type (Braun 1950), dominated by white oak in the valley floor. Along the Armuchee Ridges, an oak-pine forest dominates, with the major components including white oak, loblolly pine (*Pinus taeda*), red oak, post oak, sweet gum (*Liquidambar styraciflua*), and mockernut hickory (*Carya alba*). Lower elevations of the Armuchee Ridges and upper terraces in the valley are covered in the oak-hickory forest where rock chestnut oak (*Q. prinus*), pignut hickory (*C. glabra*), black oak (*Q. velutina*), red maple (*Acer rebrum*), and Virginia pine (*Pinus virginiana*) dominate (Wharton *op. cit.*:117). Apparently, chestnut once grew in some parts of the Ridge and Valley province (Wharton *op. cit.*:115). In the Chickamauga Valley portion of the province, cedar glades occur on low, flat limestone ridges. These unique environments are dominated by red cedar (*Juniperus virginiana*) (Wharton *op. cit.*:119).

The northern part of the Chickamauga Valley is drained by Chickamauga Creek, which empties into the Tennessee River near Chattanooga. The southern portion of this valley is drained by the Chatooga and Coosa Rivers, which empty into the Alabama. The rest of the Ridge and Valley Province in Georgia is drained almost entirely by the Coosa River and its main tributary, the Oostanaula.

Blue Ridge Province

The Blue Ridge Province in Georgia represents the terminus of the Southern Appalachian mountains. This area of Georgia contains the most rugged terrain of the state, as well as the highest peaks. Among the latter is Brasstown Bald, at 4,768 feet

A scene in the Blue Ridge Mountains. *(Courtesy U.S. Forest Service, Chattahoochee National Forest)* **Photo No. 5**

above sea level; it is Georgia's highest point. The mountains are divided into two ranges, the Blue Ridge on the east and the Cohuttas to the west. The area is underlain by igneous and metamorphic rocks of great age, for the Appalachians are among the most ancient mountains on earth. Quartzite, widely used by prehistoric peoples, is common in the area, and marble is present, mostly in a narrow belt in the Elijay and Murphy Valleys (Keith in LaForge *op. cit.*:120). Soapstone and mica are found in some areas, gold is present in the Dahlonega area, and copper is found on the Ducktown Plateau in the vicinity of the Tennessee/North Carolina state lines.

The forests of this province exhibit quite a variety of types based on elevation, soil type, moisture, and other factors. Moist, cool, north-facing mountain slopes may contain several northern hardwood species (Wharton *op. cit.*:126) representing relict communities. In the lower elevations (ca. 1500-3000 ft.), the broadleaf deciduous-hemlock forest predominates. This forest community is characterized by hemlock (*Tsuga* sp.), poplar (*Liriodendron tulipifera*), basswood (*Tilia heterophylla*), and buckeye (*Aesculus* sp.), and is generally present at the lower end of mountain coves. The upper portion of these coves (over ca. 3500 ft.) is generally covered in the broadleaf deciduous cove forest where yellow birch (*Betula lutea*), beech (*Fagus* sp.), northern red oak (*Q. borealis*), buckeye, black birch (*Betula lenta*), and poplar are often found (Wharton p. 128). Formerly, chestnut was a component of this forest type.

Along the mountain ridges at higher elevations are stands of northern red oak, and in some areas the highest peaks are mostly devoid of trees. These are the "balds" known throughout the Southern mountains, and they often contain huckleberries (*Vaccinium* spp. and *Gaylusaccia* spp.) and raspberries (*Rubus odoratus*). On ridges, at moderate elevations, the American chestnut was once the dominant species (Wharton p. 132). The lower ridges and slopes in this province are covered in the oak-hickory forest, which sometimes ranges up to 4,000 feet on south-facing slopes. The chestnut oak is a dominant species, along with scarlet oak (*Q. coccinae*), tulip poplar, white oak, northern red oak, black oak, and several species of hickory. Again, chestnut was once a component.

The Blue Ridge Province in Georgia is drained by the Little Tennessee, Hiawassee, and Toccoa Rivers (emptying into the Tennessee River or its major tributaries), the Coosawattee and Etowah (which form the Coosa River), the Chattahoochee (which empties into the Gulf), and the Tugalo (one of the main tributaries of the Savannah River).

Piedmont Plateau Province

The Piedmont Plateau of Georgia can actually be divided into several regions on the basis of topography. Bounded on the north by the Blue Ridge Province, on the northwest by the Ridge and Valley Province, and on the south by the Coastal Plain, it comprises some 31% of the state (see Map 1). The high, inner edge of the Piedmont is known as the Dahlonega Plateau and its elevation ranges from 1,800 feet above sea level where it meets the mountains to some 1,400 feet where it merges with the smoother Atlanta Plateau. The Dahlonega Plateau is in general a hilly region containing numerous residual mountains (or monadnocks) that stand above the general level. Stream valleys tend to be deep, although the eastern end of this feature is less sharply dissected and contains some rather broad valleys. The Atlanta Plateau, on the other hand, is a broadly rolling area with only a few monadnocks, among them being Stone Mountain. Southwest of the Atlanta Plateau, the land rises to a fairly rugged area known as the Tallapoosa Upland, which becomes almost mountainous along its western margin in Alabama (LaForge 1925:61).

The lower portion of the Piedmont Plateau is known as the Midlands. The topography of this area can be described as gently rolling, and in some places there are great expanses of nearly level land. Stream valleys of the main rivers tend to be fairly deep, particularly near the Fall Line. The entire Piedmont is underlain by igneous and metamorphic rocks. Quartzite is ubiquitous, soapstone is more or less locally common, and there are outcrops of basalt in a few areas.

Practically the entire Piedmont of Georgia was originally covered in oak-hickory forest, where white oak, black oak, southern red oak, pignut hickory, post oak, blackjack oak, mockernut hickory, and shagbark hickory (*Carya ovata*) are among the most common tree species. Formerly, the chestnut grew in the Piedmont as well.

The western portion of the Piedmont is drained by streams flowing into the Coosa and Chattahoochee Rivers, as well as some which empty into the Tallapoosa River. The remainder is drained by the Ocmulgee, Flint, Oconee, and Savannah Rivers and their tributaries.

Coastal Plain Province

All that portion of Georgia south of the Fall Line is included in the Coastal Plain Province and comprises over half of the total area of the state. The Fall Line, marking the boundary between the Coastal Plain and Piedmont is an obvious geologic feature, for the granitic rocks of the Piedmont end and the sedimentary rocks of the Coastal Plain begin. However, the boundary is not so obvious geographically, for the low, rolling hills of the lower Piedmont extend into the Coastal Plain for a few miles. Waterfalls are numerous along the "fall line" and gave rise to the name for this feature. The Fall Line lies roughly along a line connecting the cities of Columbus, Macon, and Augusta.

At several times in earth history, the Coastal Plain has been covered by the sea. Wharton (1978:164) best describes it:

"The Coastal Plain has been covered by successive inundations of the sea. Numerous fossil localities yield whale bones, shark teeth, and marine shells across the breadth of it. The greatest of these inundations occurred during the last epoch of the age of Dinosaurs, the Cretaceous, which left great quantities of marine sands and clays that we now call the Fall Line Sand Hills. The seashore has withdrawn further during each successive inundation, so that as we drive from Macon to Brunswick we cross younger and younger sea floors and, sometimes, the remnants of old beaches and dune systems."

The Coastal Plain of Georgia is physiographically varied. Along the Atlantic coast, the mainland is broken into peninsulas by salt marshes and tidal rivers. Offshore are the coastal islands, and inland from the coast many swamps occur. Among the latter is the Okefenokee, the second largest swamp in the United States. The coastal flatlands are replaced by a feature known as the Tifton Uplands, a region of gently rolling hills and broad, flat river valleys (Fenneman *op. cit.*:40; Cooke in LaForge 1925). This feature grades into the Fall Line Red Hills along its northern limit and into the Limesink region to the west (see Wharton *op. cit.*:9). The extremely varied natural environments of each of these regions within the Coastal Plain have been described in Wharton (*op. cit.*).

The Coastal Plain is underlain by sandstone, limestone, and other sedimentary rocks. Several types of chert occur here, and these were widely exploited by aboriginal tribes of the area (see Goad *op. cit.*).

Perhaps most of the Coastal Plain was originally covered in a mixed hardwood forest. Common species growing in the region at present include beech, water oak (*Q. nigra*), swamp chestnut oak (*Q. michauxii*), water hickory (*C. aquatica*), cypress (*Taxodium* sp.), white oak, laurel oak (*Q. laurifolia*), mockernut hickory, spruce pine (*Pinus glabra*), shortleaf pine (*P. Echinata*), and turkey oak (*Q. laevis*). Along the coast, tree species include red bay (*persea barbonia*), sweet bay (*Magnolia virginiana*), cabbage palm (*Sabal palmetto*), live oak, red cedar (*Juniperus virginiana*), slash pine (*P. elliottii*), and other species. Many unique environments occur in the Coastal Plain, and it is not our purpose to study each in detail. Rather, the above tree species give some indication of those species most often found in the Coastal Plain, and does not take into account local or areal differences in soil type, moisture, etc.

The Coastal Plain is drained principally by streams flowing into the Savannah, Ogeechee, Oconee, Ocmulgee, Flint, and Chattahoochee Rivers. Those streams originating in the Coastal Plain tend to have clear or amber-colored water, the latter because of fine particles of decayed vegetable matter. The rivers which flow out of the Piedmont and through the Coastal Plain, however, bear a heavy load of silt (Cooke in La Forge 1925).

Fauna

The forests of Georgia, with their many varieties of nut-bearing trees, afforded an abundance of animal life. The largest animals in recent times were the white-tailed deer (*Odocoileus virginianus*) and the eastern buffalo (*Bison bison pennsylvanicus*). The deer is and was found statewide in all environments, and was especially plentiful in early Colonial times before the fur trade and settlement led to serious depletion. The eastern buffalo, now extinct, was present in Georgia during the Colonial period. In this regard, Francis Moore wrote the following concerning St. Simon's Island in 1735: [St. Simon's Island] . . . "abounds with deer and rabbits; there are no buffaloes in it, though there are large herds upon the main" (Moore 1840:117). The black bear (*Ursus americanus*) was also found statewide, but is now restricted to only a few areas (see Golley 1962). The raccoon (*Procyon lotor*), opossum (*Didelphis marsupialis*), and gray squirrel (*Sciurus carolinensis*) are found statewide. Four species of rabbits are found in Georgia: the cottontail rabbit (*Sylvilagus floridanus*), found in uplands,

The white-tailed deer was the primary source of meat for Indians in Georgia for thousands of years. *(Courtesy Georgia Mountains Area Planning and Development Commission)* Photo No. 6

particularly old fields; the cane-cutter (*S. aquaticus*), found in floodplains in the Piedmont, Ridge and Valley, and upper Coastal Plain Provinces; the marsh rabbit (*S. pabustris*), found throughout the Coastal Plain; and the wood rabbit (*S. transitionalis*), found in the Blue Ridge Province and occasionally in the upper Piedmont (see Golley *op. cit.*). The woodchuck or groundhog (*Marmota monax*), is common in the mountains and upper Piedmont, and the fox squirrel (*Sciurus niger*) is found statewide, but is most common in the Coastal Plain and lower Piedmont. The wolf, mountain lion, and probably elk, were found in Georgia in early Colonial times.

The largest and economically the most important bird in Georgia in the early historic period was the wild turkey (*Malleagris gallopavo*). Found throughout the state, it was especially common in areas where acorns abounded. Shelford (1963:59) speculates that the wild turkey may have had its largest populations in the oak-hickory forest because of the abundance of acorns. Georgia is not considered as being in one of the major flyways or migration routes of migratory waterfowl. Nevertheless, some wild ducks, geese, and swans can be found in the state during the winter months (Burleigh 1958). The ruffed grouse (*Bonasa umbrellus monticola*) is fairly common in the mountains and portions of the upper Piedmont, while the bobwhite (*Colinus virginianus*) is found throughout the state. The now-extinct passenger pigeon once wintered in the state. Aside from these birds, Georgia has a wide variety of smaller species of little or no economic significance to native tribes of the area.

The wild turkey was the most important game bird to Georgia's native peoples. *(Courtesy Georgia Mountains Area Planning and Development Commission)* **Photo No. 7**

Georgia's aquatic life, both marine and freshwater, formed valuable food resources for native peoples. The rivers and creeks of the state abounded in fish of many species, including catfish (*Ictalurus* spp.), pickerel (*Esox* spp.), sturgeon (*Acipensea* spp.), the American shad (*Alosa sapidissima*), and others. Other freshwater resources included the snapping turtle (*Chelydra serpentina*), American eel (*Anguilla rostrata*), and freshwater mussels (*Unionidae* spp.). Along the coast, the varieties of fish, shellfish, molluscs, etc. are too numerous to list in this work (see Dahlberg 1975), but it should be noted that several varieties of whales sometimes beach along the Georgia coast. Finally, the manatee (*Trichechus manatus*) can be seen along the coast in sheltered bays or sluggish rivers.

Conclusion

The significance of the foregoing will become evident later in this work, for the presence of certain significant resources had a direct bearing on seasonal movements of prehistoric populations whose livelihood was based on hunting, fishing, and gathering. This was particularly true of Archaic peoples (8,000-1,000 B.C.), who widely exploited edible nuts, berries, birds, fish, mammals, reptiles, and probably edible roots, tubers, and greens. Furthermore, the availability of certain types of raw material was important. Stone such as chert and basalt are not found widely in Georgia, but were much in demand by early inhabitants of the area. Thus, the presence of these, and other materials on an archaeological site in an area where they do not occur naturally may indicate trade between prehistoric peoples living in different parts of the state or nearby states.

The presence of plant or animal remains on a site can indicate the season during which early peoples lived at that precise location. The heavy dependence on hunting, gathering, and fishing, particularly before agriculture appears, generally required the people to move on a seasonal basis. A group might live in or near the riverbottoms during the spring and early summer in order to pick berries, gather edible greens, and fish. Fishing was probably a very important activity along streams where migratory fish, such as the American shad, appeared in annual "runs." During the fall, this same group of people might move into the uplands to gather acorns, hickory nuts, and other nuts, as well as to hunt the birds and animals there to feed on the mast. Artifacts at the various sites can indicate some of the activities which occurred at each site. For instance, the presence of netsinkers and fishhooks indicate fishing; mortars and pestles suggest that some kind of seed or nuts were being processed; an abundance of stone knives, scrapers and projectile points may indicate a hunting camp, etc. Therefore, a study of the artifacts found on a site, the location of the site, and knowledge of natural resources in the immediate vicinity of the site can tell us quite a lot about the life of Georgia's early inhabitants.

However, Georgia's first human inhabitants were faced with a situation very different from that just described. They did not have the abundance of natural food sources which later peoples had, because the climate was much colder. Consequently, animals, birds, and nut-bearing trees so important to later peoples were either not present at all or were restricted to only a few areas where their survival was possible. The Pleistocene environment and Georgia's earliest people are discussed in the following chapter.

REFERENCES: CHAPTER II

Braun, E. Lucy, *Deciduous Forests of Eastern North America,* Hafner Publishing Co., New York.
1967

Burleigh, Thomas D., *Georgia Birds,* University of Oklahoma Press, Norman.
1958

Dahlberg, Michael D., *Guide to Coastal Fishes of Georgia and Nearby States,* University of Georgia
1975   Press, Athens.

Fenneman, Nevin M., *Physiography of Eastern United States,* McGraw-Hill Book Co., Inc., New
1938   York.

Goad, Sharon I., *Chert Resources in Georgia: Archaeological and Geological Perspectives,* Uni-
1979   versity of Georgia Laboratory of Archaeology Series, No. 21, Athens.

Golley, Frank B., *Mammals of Georgia,* University of Georgia Press, Athens.
1962

LaForge, Laurence, et. al., *Physical Geography of Georgia,* Geological Survey of Georgia, Bulletin
1925   No. 42, Atlanta.

Lee, David S., et al., *Atlas of North American Freshwater Fishes,* North Carolina State Museum of
1980   Natural History, Raleigh.

Miller, Robert A., *The Geologic History of Tennessee,* State of Tennessee, Department of Conser-
1974   vation, Division of Geology, Nashville.

Moore, Francis, "A Voyage to Georgia, Begun in the Year 1735," in *Collections of the Georgia*
1840   *Historical Society,* Vol. 1, Savannah.

Shelford, Victor E., *The Ecology of North America,* University of Illinois Press, Urbana.
1963

Thornbury, William D., *Regional Geomorphology of the United States,* John Wiley and Sons, Inc.,
1965   New York.

Wharton, Charles H., *The Natural Environments of Georgia,* Georgia Department of Natural Re-
1978   sources, Atlanta.

Chapter III

THE PALEO-INDIAN
AND
TRANSITIONAL PERIOD

*I*n the foregoing chapter, the current (and historic) regional diversity in Georgia's plant and animal species was discussed. While this variety presented the historic Indian tribes with an abundance of natural foods with which to supplement their agricultural produce, the state's earliest inhabitants were presented with a far different situation. The area of what is now Georgia during the late Pleistocene would hardly have been recognizable to later peoples, for both plant and animal species were different from those familiar to us today. Since the state's first human inhabitants were hunters and gatherers, an understanding of what the environment was like is crucial to any interpretation of the activities of early man. Fortunately, the research of geologists and palynologists in Georgia and neighboring states now permits a more complete reconstruction of the late Pleistocene environment than has heretofore been the case.

The Pleistocene, the last major time period in earth's history, began some two to five million years ago. It has been described as a most unusual period in geologic history because of the extreme climatic fluctuations which occurred. The Pleistocene was marked by alternating periods of extreme cold, evidenced by the formation of huge continental glaciers, and temperate periods during which the glaciers retreated and the climate became warmer. Events surrounding the final glacial episode, termed the Wisconsin glaciation, are of utmost importance, for it was probably sometime during this period that man arrived in the New World.

The Wisconsin glaciation began about 100,000 years ago and lasted until about 12,000 years ago. It was marked by several fluctuations, i.e., advances and retreats of the ice mass. The Winconsin glacier covered almost all of northern North America and at its maximum extent, it reached as far south as central Indiana and Ohio (see Map 2). Of primary concern is the final major advance of the ice, termed the Woodfordian substage, which began about 23,000 years ago (Butzer 1971:354). This last advance was preceded by a rather warm period known as the Farmdale interstadial, which lasted from about 29,000 years ago to about 23,000 years ago. Evidence indicates however, that the climate was deteriorating toward the end of this interstadial, setting the stage for the glacial re-advance. This last major ice advance was again accompanied by marked shifts in plant and animal communities. The Woodfordian substage ended about 12,800 years ago (Butzer *ibid.*), with the maximum advance of the ice mass

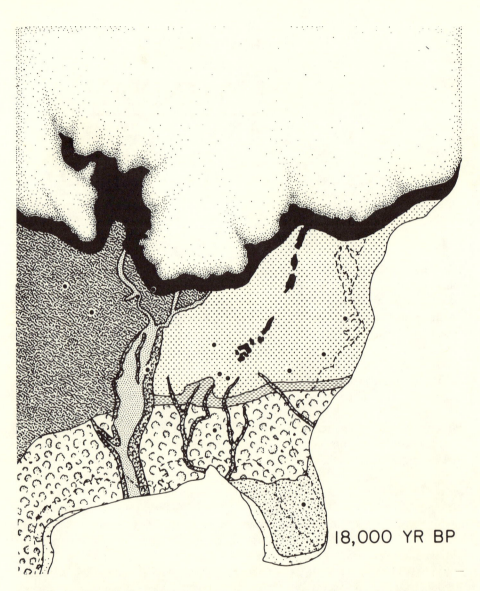

18,000 YR BP

Vegetation zones of the Eastern United States 18,000 years before present. *(Courtesy Paul A. Delcourt)* **Map 2.**

occurring about 18,000 years ago (Flint 1971:463). This substage was followed by another warming trend, the Two Creeks interstadial, which lasted until about 11,500 years ago. A minor advance of the ice mass, the Valders substage, began about 11,500 years ago but was short-lived. There is evidence that retreat was already well underway by about 10,750 years ago, and the glacier had already retreated northward out of the continental United States by 10,000 years ago (Butzer *op. cit.*:355). Following this substage, a rather rapid warming trend set in which culminated in the establishment of plant and animal communities more or less typical of the present time in Georgia.

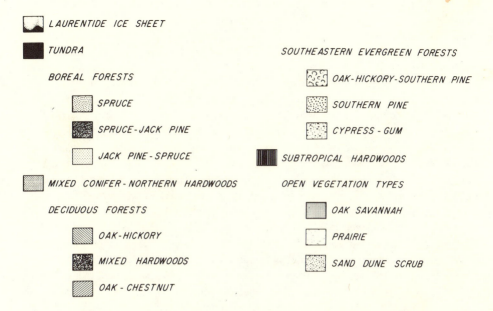

LAURENTIDE ICE SHEET

TUNDRA

SOUTHEASTERN EVERGREEN FORESTS

BOREAL FORESTS

OAK-HICKORY-SOUTHERN PINE

SPRUCE

SOUTHERN PINE

SPRUCE-JACK PINE

CYPRESS - GUM

JACK PINE - SPRUCE

SUBTROPICAL HARDWOODS

MIXED CONIFER - NORTHERN HARDWOODS

OPEN VEGETATION TYPES

DECIDUOUS FORESTS

OAK SAVANNAH

OAK-HICKORY

PRAIRIE

MIXED HARDWOODS

SAND DUNE SCRUB

OAK - CHESTNUT

With each major advance of the ice mass, there were corresponding retreats southward of plant and animal communities. Studies of fossil pollen at several locales throughout the Southeast demonstrate the presence of flora more typical of present-day Canada and the northernmost United States. This research centers on the last 30,000 years and is thus of direct relevance to the study of early man in the area.

The primary means of reconstructing past environments is through palynology — the study of ancient plant pollen and spores. Most plants shed their pollen, which is as distinctive as the plant's leaves, and the wind disperses and deposits this pollen over a wide area. Microscopic analysis of pollen samples from any given layer in an archaeological site or core sample from lake bottom sediments can give a good indication of the kinds of plants growing in the vicinity when the layer was formed. Swamps, bogs, and natural ponds and lakes form ideal conditions for pollen preservation and it is from the stratified sediments in these natural features that some of the best evidence for climatic change in the Southeast is obtained. Currently, palynologists have a reasonably good idea of southeastern forest types extending back to about 30,000 B.P. (Before Present), a date more or less coinciding with the rather warm Farmdale interstadial (ca. 29,000-23,000 B.P.). Some of the sites where this information has been obtained are in Georgia.

Pollen studies carried out on sediments from the Green Pond, in Bartow County, indicate that prior to ca. 30,000 B.P., the area was rather dry and was covered in a pine forest. However, increasing rainfall apparently led to the re-establishment of the deciduous forest in this part of northwest Georgia, for pond sediments reveal the presence of oak (*Quercus* sp.) and hickory (*Carya* sp.) pollen, along with small amounts of pine (*Pinus* sp.) and swamp cypress (*Taxodium*) (Watts 1973:261). At about 25,000 B.P., the incidence of pine and sweetgum (*Liquidambar*) increases, and this

21

along with other indications points to an increasingly colder climate (Watts *op. cit.*: 263). This change in the incidence of certain forest species apparently reflects the climatic and vegetational changes accompanying the final major ice advance, the Woodfordian substage.

Beginning ca. 23,000 B.P. (Butzer 1971:354), the Woodfordian substage saw another advance of the ice mass, a movement which reached its peak about 18,000 B.P. when the ice reached its southernmost extent. This colder climate is recorded in the pollen sequence at two other natural ponds in Bartow County. Basal deposits at the Quicksand Pond and the Bob Black Pond yield Carbon-14 dates of 20,100 B.P. and 22,900 B.P., respectively (Watts 1970:17). Pollen from this basal zone includes that of dwarf mistletow (*Arceuthobium*), which does not presently grow south of New Jersey (Watts *op. cit.*:23). The normal host of this species is black spruce (*Picea mariana*), and Watts speculates that the unidentifiable spruce pollen from this zone is probably that of the black spruce (*ibid.*). Watts further notes that species of diatoms, certain types of algae with silicified cell walls, represented in this deposit are similar to the diatom assemblage in lakes of northeastern Minnesota at the present time. The succeeding zone in both ponds yielded pollen from aquatic plants which today grow in New England and the Great Lakes region. Also present is the pollen of jackpine (*Pinus banksiana*), a species now found mainly in the Canadian boreal forest (Watts *op. cit.*:25). Carbon-14 dates on organic matter from the base of this zone indicated an age of about 20,100 B.P., while the top of the zone yielded a date of 13,500 B.P. (*ibid.*).

Elsewhere in the Southeast, studies in Virginia and the Carolinas give further indications of the kinds of forests found in the area during the final glacial epoch. Apparently, southeastern North Carolina was characterized by scattered pine and spruce trees in a very open, savanna-like situation (Whitehead 1967:237). At the same time, southeastern Virginia seems to have been covered in a forest composed primarily of spruce, but also containing some pine and fir trees (*ibid.*). Pollen studies indicate that in late glacial times, the pine and spruce varieties were replaced by oak, hickory, beech, hemlock, birch, and alder (*op. cit.*:238).

This replacement of the pine-spruce forest is also evident in the South Carolina coastal plain, at the White Pond. The zone dated 19,100-12,810 B.P. at this site exhibits a pollen diagram indicating pine (*Pinus banksiana*) as the dominant species, with both red spruce (*Picea rubens*) and white spruce (*Picea glauca*) being present (Watts 1980:189). By about 15,000 B.P., however, oak (*Quercus* sp.) and hickory (*Carya* sp.) had begun to invade the area, and the succeeding zone in pond sediments, dated at 12,810-9,550 B.P., indicates a steep decline in the percentage of pine pollen and the disappearance of spruce pollen. It was during this time that the deciduous forest returned to the area, but after ca. 9,550 B.P., many deciduous varieties declined in number and were replaced by southern pine varieties. By ca. 7,000 B.P., a predominantly modern forest, dominated by pine, was established (Watts *op. cit.*: 195).

Basically, the same sequence of events is recorded in the pollen from a small marsh on Lookout Mountain in northwest Georgia. There is evidence that pine and spruce grew here until about 10,820 B.P., but by 10,500 B.P. a mixed deciduous forest, with beech as a major component, dominated. The succeeding zone yields pollen of an essentially modern forest (Watts 1975:287, 290).

These and other studies now permit a reconstruction of the forest types predominating in the Southeast during the past 30,000 years. With the climate changes accompanying the final glacial advance, vegetation zones shifted southward and by 18,000 B.P., a date coinciding with the maximum glaciation, the oak-hickory-southern pine forest was displaced southward to the coastal plain of Georgia, and extended westward into Texas (see Map 2, page 20; also see Davis 1976:15). To the north, a jackpine-spruce-fir forest covered the Piedmont and Appalachians, with tundra probably being present in the highest elevations of the mountains. A forest of poplar, oak, chestnut, and other species (see Shelford 1964:35) evidently occupied stream margins in the coastal plain and into the lower Piedmont. Northward on the Atlantic coastal plain of the Carolinas, the oak-hickory woodland was replaced by jackpine-spruce woodland (Delcourt and Delcourt 1979:96).

With climatic amelioration, the deciduous forest began expanding northward beginning ca. 16,500 B.P. (Delcourt and Delcourt *op. cit.*:97), and had replaced the predominantly jackpine forest by ca. 12,500 B.P. in the Southeast. Changes continued to occur in forest composition, however, with southern pine forests ultimately replacing the deciduous forest on the uplands of the Gulf coastal plain (Delcourt 1980:385). By ca. 5,000 B.P., the modern distribution of forest types in the Southeast was established (*op. cit.*:384). The southeastern forests of this transitional period (ca. 16,500-10,000 B.P.) were unlike any forests of the present time, for tree species found today far to the north were growing in proximity to southern tree varieties. Watts (1975: 291; 1980:192) notes that the tree assemblages of this time have no modern counterparts. The fossil evidence indicates that this same situation is also true for faunal species which inhabited the Southeast during this time.

The late Pleistocene saw the widespread distribution of exotic life forms, and near the end of the period, the extinction of many species. The displacement of animal populations during glacial advances can be demonstrated through the fossil record, just as the displacement of forest types can be demonstrated through palynology. Faunal remains of late Pleistocene affinity have been recovered in all the southeastern states, and these fossils serve to demonstrate the presence of a wide variety of species.

In Georgia, a locale in Glynn County, on the coastal plain, has yielded the fossil remains of some late Pleistocene species. The remains have yielded Carbon-14 dates which average ca. 10,000 B.P., a time when the area was probably covered in mixed oak-hickory-southern pine forest. The species represented here include the giant ground sloth (*Eremotherium*), horse (*Equus cf. conversidens*), tapir (*Tapirus*), deer (*Odocoileus*), and mammoth (*Mammuthus* sp.) (Voorhies 1971:128). To the north, a location in Wilkes County has yielded one of the best fossil assemblages yet discovered in the Piedmont. The fossil deposit, located on Little Kettle Creek, is believed to date from full-glacial times (Voorhies 1974:85). The Piedmont at that time was covered by a jackpine-spruce forest, as was demonstrated above, and stream margins may have supported deciduous varieties in the lower Piedmont. The faunal evidence at this location corroborates the palynological evidence of a much cooler climate. Species which indicate a radically different climate include the southern bog lemming (*Synaptomys cooperi* B.) and the red-backed vole (*Clethrionomys* sp.). Both are rodents which are found mainly in northern coniferous forests, but range southward into the highest elevations of the Southern Appalachians at the present time. The remains of the red-backed vole in Wilkes County is the southernmost occurrence of this species on record and strongly suggests much cooler conditions in the Georgia Piedmont at the time of deposition (Voorhies 1974). In addition, remains of mastodon (*Mammut americanum*), mammoth (*Mammuthus* sp.), bison (*Bison* sp.), and white-tailed deer (*Odocoileus virginiana*) were recovered from the same deposit (*ibid.*). The presence of bison and mammoth here leads one to speculate on whether there were grassy areas in the Piedmont at this time. Perhaps groves or clumps of trees were separated by grasslands or perhaps the ridgetops in exposed areas were covered in grasses. At any rate, the presence of grazing animals in a continuous coniferous forest seems unlikely.

In Bartow County, northwest Georgia, remains of ground sloth (*Megalonyx* sp.), southern bog lemming (*Synaptomys cooperi* B.), North American spectacled bear (*Trimarctus floridanus*), and horse (*Equus* sp.) were found in Pleistocene deposits on Quarry Mountain (Ray 1967:121). In addition, remains of the spruce grouse (*Canarch-ites canadenis*), a species found today in northern coniferous forests from Alaska and Canada southward into northern Wisconsin, Vermont, and Maine, were recovered from this site (Wetmore 1967:151). To these finds may be added a mammoth tooth found in Bartow County in 1950 and a tapir mandible fragment found in Walker County (northwest Georgia) in 1955 (Lipps and Ray 1967:113).

Elsewhere in the Southeast, the remains of Pleistocene fauna have been recovered from various locations. Florida is especially rich in fossils of this period and one locale in Levy County has yielded remains of ground sloth, dire wolf, North American spectacled bear, jaguar, saber-toothed cat, American mastodon, horse, and peccary, all dating to ca. 10,000 B.P. (Martin and Webb 1974). One writer has noted that evidence also indicates the presence of bison (*Bison antiquus*) in Florida during this time. In South Carolina, moose and walrus remains have been recovered along the coast in a late Pleistocene context (Blair 1958:436), and musk ox remains have been found as far south as Mississippi (*ibid*).

In addition to these finds, information concerning the distribution and presumed habits of late Pleistocene fauna in the Southeast can be found in an article by Martin and Guilday (in Martin and Wright 1967). According to this source, at least two species of ground sloth, *Megalonyx* N. and *Eremotherium* S., inhabited the Southeast. *Megalonyx* is considered to have been a woodland or forest dweller. *Eremotherium* was as tall as modern giraffs (see Fig. 2). Other species making up the faunal assemblage of the late Pleistocene in the Southeast include the capybara (*Neochoerus* Hay), glyptodon (*Boreostracon floridanus*), tapir (*Tapirus* sp.), long-nosed peccary (*Mylohyus* Cope), and in the northern part of the Southeast, the woodland musk ox (*Bootherium* Leidy) (Martin and Guilday *op. cit.*).

The overall picture presented by the foregoing data is that of a varied flora and fauna forming assemblages with no modern counterparts. Apparently, the jackpine-spruce woodland or parkland covering a large portion of the Southeast during the late Pleistocene contained a much more varied animal population than is the case in modern boreal or spruce-fir forests (see Shelford 1963:124-136). Remains of this late Pleistocene fauna are most numerous in the coastal plain, where parkland or savanna may have been the predominant ground cover. It is probably no mere coincidence that some of the earliest evidence of human presence in the Southeast is found in precisely this same area.

Georgia's Earliest People

The date of the appearance of man in the New World is unknown and probably will never be known. It has been established, however, that early man reached the Western Hemisphere via the Bering Strait land bridge. Several times during the last 100,000 years, a strip of land approximately 1,200 miles wide existed between what is now Alaska and Siberia (Haag 1973). The exposure of this vast plain was due to a lowering of sea level which in turn was due to the tremendous amount of moisture being locked up in the huge continental glaciers of North America and northern Europe and Asia. Over this land bridge between the continents passed a variety of animal life, including man.

Evidence of man's presence in North America has been firmly established back to about 15,000 years ago. There is very good evidence for human presence here prior to that time, but until recently, there were no firmly established dates nor evidence of an indisputable nature. However, a recent find in California seems to demonstrate human presence there at least 50,000 years ago (Childers and Minshall 1980: 297).

Central in the discussion of man's antiquity in the New World is evidence for a so-called "pre-projectile point horizon," a time in New World prehistory when crude stone tools were used, but apparently the techniques for manufacturing bifacially flaked tools had not developed. Those who adhere to this idea base their arguments on the existence of crude, percussion-flaked tools identified as scrapers, flakes, and pebble-choppers (see Willey 1966:29). Such tool assemblages do not contain bifacially flaked projectile points or knives. Some such artifacts have been found in apparent association with Pleistocene faunal remains, but as yet, no indisputable association has come to light. Most artifacts of this type represent surface finds, but still, bifacially chipped projectile points are missing. This has been interpreted as representing a flaking technology brought over from the Old World, out of which bifacially worked projectile points had not yet developed. Another possibility deserves mention, however, and that is that projectile points may have been fashioned from perishable material, i.e., wood or bone. The use of bone projectile points by Paleo-Indians during the time when the well-known Folsom points were being made is well documented (see Frison and Zeimens 1980), and the use of wood, bone, deer antler, and wild turkey spurs as projectile points by historic southeastern tribes is also well documented (see Swanton 1946; et al.). Thus, the stone tools interpreted as belonging to a "pre-projectile point horizon" may represent processing tools and may not necessarily indicate the absence of projectile points.

One artifact assemblage from Alabama deserves mention at this point, for it has been interpreted by some as evidence for the pre-projectile point era. The artifacts in question belong to the so-called Lively Complex, named for its discoverer, Matthew Lively. The tools are described as being made from quartz pebbles, and they exhibit rather crude chipping techniques, with the removal of a large flake on one surface to make a striking platform, then the removal of a few flakes on the opposite side to form a cutting edge (see Lively 1965). Also found on the same sites which produced these choppers were "pebble-drills," artifacts with thick cross-sections and with definite wear marks on the tip. The author of the article is careful to avoid assigning a date to these artifacts, for all represent surface finds and (more importantly) all are found on sites where artifacts belonging to the Paleo-Indian and later time periods have also been found. Lively does speculate, however, that since these crude tools have not been found associated with known archaeological assemblages elsewhere, they must belong to a period chronologically considerably removed from these known assemblages (*op. cit.*:122). While artifacts of this type have been reported elsewhere in Alabama, there are as yet no known finds in Georgia. The status of the "Lively Complex" remains unknown, and discussion of it has largely disappeared from archaeological circles.

To date, the earliest evidence of man's presence in Georgia and the Southeast is in the form of fluted projectile points identical to or very similar to those found west of the Mississippi and dated to about 12,000 years ago. The fluted points found in Georgia and surrounding states are assumed to be contemporary with those of the West on the basis of typology, for practically none has been found *in situ* and thus cannot be dated by Carbon-14 or other methods. The earliest descriptions of these artifacts in Georgia refer to them as Folsom or "Folsomoid" points, due to their similarity to points from the Folsom site in New Mexico then being publicized. However, the southeastern fluted points more closely resemble the Clovis points, which were discovered a few years later than Folsom. Wormington, in her classic work on the earliest human inhabitants of North America, describes Clovis points as fluted lanceolate projectile points with parallel or slightly convex sides and concave bases, and ranging from one and one-half to five inches in length. Usually, they are about three inches in length. The flutes sometimes extend almost the full length, but the usual pattern is for the flute to extend no more than half way from the base to the tip. Also, there is evidence of basal grinding in most instances. The Cumberland point, a southeastern variant, is described as being like the Clovis point except that it is constricted at the base, creating a fish-tailed effect (Wormington 1957:263).

Clovis points, along with snub-nosed stone scrapers, flake knives, and bone points, have been found associated with the remains of extinct Pleistocene megafauna at several sites west of the Mississippi (Wormington *op. cit.*:43-59); Haynes 1966; Willey 1966; et al.). At the Blackwater Draw site in New Mexico, these points were found in direct association with mammoth, camel, horse, and bison remains, and Carbon-14 dates place the Clovis level at about 9,200 B.C. (Willey *op. cit.*:40). At the Lehner site in New Mexico, a total of thirteen Clovis projectile points were found along with butchering tools among the bones of nine young mammoths (Haynes *op. cit.*). Again, Carbon-14 dates indicate an age of slightly earlier than 9,000 B.C. Only one find is known from the eastern United States where a Clovis point has been found associated with the remains of extinct fauna, and this discovery was made recently in the Kimmswick bone beds of Mastodon State Park near St. Louis, Missouri (Anonymous 1979).

As has been demonstrated earlier in this chapter, remains of mammoth and other Pleistocene fauna have been found at several localities in Georgia and surrounding states, but as yet no human artifacts have been found in association with these remains. Despite this fact, archaeologists generally believe that the Clovis and related projectile point types in the Southeast are at least as old as those forms found in the West and that they were contemporary with the extinct life forms mentioned above.

Fluted points have been found in most areas of Georgia, but almost always on the ground surface or in a situation where re-deposition has occurred (Caldwell

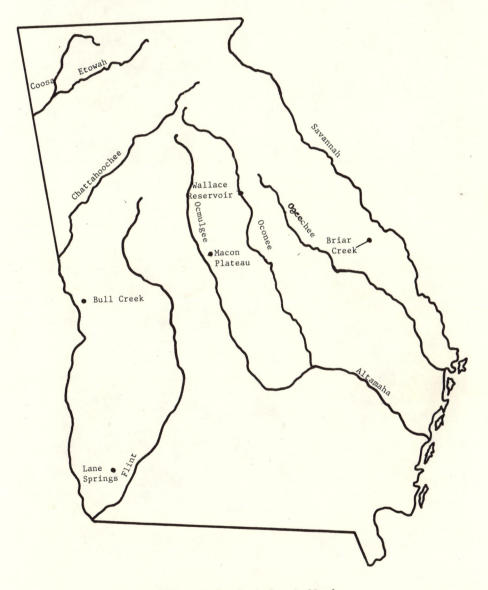

Some Paleo-Indian sites in Georgia. Map 3.

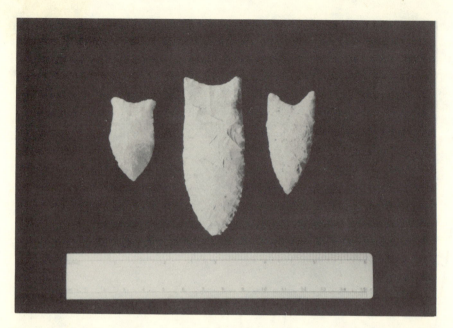

Paleo-Indian fluted points from Georgia. Specimen on left is from northwest Georgia, others are from Calhoun County. *(From a private collection)* Photo No. 8

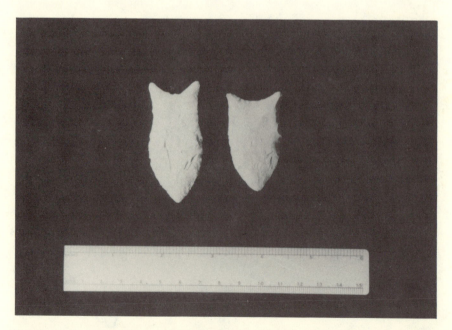

Paleo-Indian fluted points from Georgia. Specimen on left is from Calhoun County; specimen on right is from Terrell County. *(From a private collection)* Photo No. 9

1952; Fairbanks 1952). Perhaps the first *in situ* find made in Georgia was that made by A.R. Kelly in the course of his excavations on the Macon Plateau in the 1930's. Along with "thousands of worked flints" which "exhibit many primitive chipping characteristics and indicate a surprising assemblage of specialized scrapers," Kelly found one fluted projectile point (Kelly 1938:2, 7). The fluted point and the associated artifacts showed advanced patination, a chemical change taking place in the surface of the stone such that over a long period of time the original coloration is lost. This artifact assemblage was found in "the deepest loams" on the site and was compared to the tool kits of the Paleo-Indians then being discovered in the West (Kelly *op. cit.*).

A similar assemblage was discovered by Kelly a few years later, but unfortunately the artifacts were not *in situ* (Kelly 1950). This site was located at Lane Springs, on upper Spring Creek, Decatur County. A flood here in 1948 washed away part of a sandy ridge bordering the creek, exposing the underlying clay. The assemblage of end scrapers, choppers, and blades revealed by the water action also included one unfluted "folsomoid" point and several projectile points characteristic of the Archaic period. These artifacts were all washed from the sandy ridge and were left exposed on the underlying clay by the floodwaters. The unfluted projectile point and the choppers and other tools typically associated with Paleo-Indian sites exhibited advanced patination comparable to those recovered from the Macon Plateau (Kelly *op. cit.*).

The WPA archaeological survey of north Georgia, carried out in 1938-40 by Robert Wauchope, recorded several Paleo-Indian artifacts from this part of the state. Wauchope (1966:99) notes that four fluted Clovis points were recorded by this survey, two of which were from Bartow County. The other two were given to members of the survey and are of unknown provenience. In addition to the fluted points, eleven points described as having all the attributes of the Clovis tradition except fluting, were recorded from sites in Bartow, Cherokee, and Morgan Counties (*ibid.*). Also found were four fluted points of the Cumberland variety on sites in Walton and Bartow Counties (*op. cit.*:100). Wauchope goes on to list a total of eighty-one projectile points which exhibit most of the attributes of Cumberland fluted points except that they lack fluting. In view of archaeological works since his time, I think it is reasonable to conclude that some of the points which Wauchope included in the latter category more properly belong with Woodland assemblages, while others are to be identified as Quad projectile point types (see Wauchope *op. cit.*: Fig. 45, p. 100).

In a survey along the Oconee River in the lower Piedmont of Georgia, Paleo-Indian remains were identified on thirty-six of the three thousand sites found prior to flooding by the Wallace reservoir (O'Steen et al. 1983). Three types of sites were noticed: small sites on the floodplain containing mostly butchering and processing tools; upland quarrying and manufacturing sites; sites along the floodplain and uplands near shoals. The latter sites contain a high diversity of tool types, and all sites contained artifacts made of both local and non-local materials. The authors of the study conclude that the Paleo-Indian occupation of the Georgia Piedmont was sparse indeed, for it made up only one percent of the sites located in the Wallace Reservoir (*op. cit.*).

Other evidence of Paleo-Indians in Georgia as discussed in the archaeological literature is sparse. One "Folsom" point is said to have been found at the Bull Creek site, near Columbus (Patterson 1950:37), and Waring notes that the museum at Washington, Georgia, has three fluted points, two of which are from Richmond County and the other from Burke County (Waring in Williams 1965b:14). Miller (1950:274) notes that fluted points had reportedly been found along Big Kiokee Creek in eastern Georgia and that the survey of the Clark Hill reservoir revealed snub-nosed scrapers comparable to those found on early man sites in the West. In a survey of the Dry Creek watershed, Clovis points and associated artifacts were found on a site located on a tributary of Dry Creek (Fish and Fish 1977:9). In another survey, a fluted point was found near the confluence of Ebenezer Creek and the Savannah River (Fish 1976:18). A private collection in North Carolina, examined by the author of this work, contains two fluted points from the Dahlonega area, and one other fluted point from near Hiawassee is in a private collection in northeast Georgia. Finally, A.R. Kelly noted that he saw several fluted points in a private collection during the 1930's, and that all the points had been found in the vicinity of Wren's, Georgia, (in Williams 1965a:14). Waring (in Williams *op. cit.*) adds that these points were from a site somewhere along the headwaters of Briar Creek and that fluted points made from flint obtained in this same area have been found as far away as the South Carolina coast.

Aside from noting the geographic position of these finds, what can be learned about the activities of Georgia's inhabitants during the late Pleistocene? One avenue of approach is to note the settlement pattern as revealed by site locations. In nearly all instances, Paleo-Indian artifacts have been found on hills or ridges overlooking streams, particularly those located at or near the confluence of two streams. Such sites must have been selected for use as a vantage point in following game movements in the valley. This same situation exists elsewhere in the eastern United States and in the Southwest, and is probably indicative of a very widespread method of hunting.

Because of the artifacts associated with the Paleo-Indian occupation, as well as the location of known sites, it is generally believed that these early inhabitants of the Southeast were wandering hunters whose primary quarry was the Pleistocene megafauna, i.e., mammoth, mastodon, ground sloth, et al. It has been noted that most of the known fluted points from North Carolina were found in the coastal plain, the same area where most of the state's mastodon remains have been found (Williams and Stoltman 1965:678). Virtually the same situation is true for South Carolina, where nearly all known fluted points in the state were found in the coastal plain and along the Fall Line (Michie 1977:87). Only a few finds are known from the Piedmont, and these are nearly all from the lower Piedmont and are associated with major rivers (*op. cit.*:94). In Florida, Paleo-Indian remains seem to cluster in the northwestern part of the state, particularly around the Santa Fe River (see Waller and Dunbar 1977). It is in and around this and other rivers, especially at shoals and other shallow areas where game trails cross, that these remains have been found. Since the remains of Pleistocene fauna abound on the riverbottoms at these locations, Waller (1970) has suggested the possibility that the early hunters attacked their quarry here.

The actual hunting methods of the Paleo-Indians have been the subject of much speculation in recent years, and the study of contemporary animals and hunting patterns has been employed in order to gain insights into ancient life. Gorman (1972), in an intriguing article, suggests that it is reasonable to study the habits of modern

African elephants in order to understand the habits of the extinct mammoth. He notes that African elephants are restricted to regions which offer water and good browsing and grazing. He further notes that when an elephant is surprised or wounded, it immediately flees to a water source, sometimes traveling several miles. Gorman argues that mammoths probably exhibited the same behavior and that the "kill" sites do not represent a complete attack-kill-butcher sequence. Rather, the mammoth was probably attacked at some distance away by one group of hunters, while others were positioned near where the game trails led to water holes or river crossings. It was here that the final phase of the hunt was carried out. This would seem to explain the existence of Paleo-Indian sites on high ground overlooking streams, valleys, stream confluences, springs, and lakes and at river crossings. Dragoo (1979:205, 207) further suggests that the animals were butchered at the kill site, but the meat was removed to a camp some distance away because of the very real danger from large Pleistocene predators who might be attracted by the smell of the blood and offal.

While there are no modern counterparts of the giant ground sloth, other species probably hunted by early man in Georgia still exist. One such animal is the tapir. The presence of the tapir in the Southeast during the late Pleistocene has been discussed earlier in this chapter, and modern representatives can be found in South America. While it generally lives near rivers or streams, the tapir can also be found in rather dry grasslands (Matthews 1971:344). Indians in the tropical forest of Bolivia lure the animal by imitating its clicks and squeals, then attempt to wound it with a special arrow designed to increase blood flow. Every effort is made not to frighten the animal, nor to give chase, but merely to track it through the forest until it expires. If frightened, it will immediately make for a stream or other water source (Mr. Paul Johnson, New Tribes Missions, personal communication).

If the stream margins of the coastal plain and lower Piedmont were the most heavily forested areas during the late Pleistocene (Michie op. cit.:118; Delcourt and Delcourt 1979), then these areas would have formed an ideal habitat for many faunal species. This, then would explain the apparent clustering of Paleo-Indian sites near rivers or other water sources. It is important to note, however, that our understanding of site distribution during this time is very incomplete, and sites may exist in other environmental situations, such as riverbottoms, but may be buried under several feet of sediments and thus remain undetected (see Williams and Stoltman op. cit.:678; et al.). It should further be noted that the stream margins would probably have provided early man with vegetal foods, particularly if nut-bearing trees grew there. It should not be assumed that the Paleo-Indians subsisted entirely on the Pleistocene megafauna and smaller animal species. Man must have vegetable foods in one form or another, but no evidence of plant utilization by Paleo-Indians has yet been discovered. Succeeding time periods, however, do yield evidence of the exploitation of plant foods, along with indications of a different way of life. The cultural changes reflected in the artifacts are believed to represent early man's adaptations to a situation he probably little understood and over which he had no control—environmental change.

The Transitional Phase

The climatic change occurring primarily between about 10,000 B.C. and about 8,000 B.C. was quite rapid and led to drastic changes in plant and animal life in the Southeast. Indeed, the climate had been moderating since about 14,500 B.C., for it was about this time that oak and hickory pollen appears in sediments in the South Carolina Piedmont (see above). However, the trend toward warmer temperatures accelerated, and resulted in northern plant and animal varieties retreating northward. The rapidity of this change is reflected in pollen studies from Lookout Mountain (already discussed) in Georgia, where spruce and pine grew at ca. 8,800 B.C., but had been replaced by a mixed deciduous forest by ca. 8,500 B.C. It was at about this time, as the vegetation zones shifted northward, that many animal species became extinct.

Several theories have been advanced to explain the Pleistocene extinctions, which occurred throughout the world. The primary species to die out included the large mammals (mammoth, mastodon, ground sloth, and others), and perhaps their adaptation to a particular environment led to their demise, as the climate was changing rapidly. There is reason to believe that some of the large mammals may have survived in Florida as late as 6,500 B.C. (Martin and Webb 1974), but they are generally thought to have disappeared from most other areas much earlier. If the Paleo-Indian peoples of Georgia and the Southeast were primarily dependent on the exploitation of this large game, then its rather rapid disappearance necessitated a shift in prey and, with the rapid appearance of the deciduous forest, a change in hunting patterns as well. This change is reflected in various artifacts recognized as belonging to the late Paleo-Indian Transitional phase.

With the extinction of the large game animals, white-tailed deer and smaller game became the dominant species in the newly established deciduous forest. This situation necessitated a change in subsistence techniques and technology on the part of the area's human inhabitants. This change is most apparent in the projectile points of the Transitional Phase (ca. 10,500 B.C.-8,000 B.C.). Several projectile point forms in the Southeast, including Suwanee, Quad, Hardaway, and Dalton, are all seen as having developed out of the fluted point tradition (Willey 1966:50; Mason 1962:239-42; et al.). Examples of each type have been found in Georgia and testify to the general trend of change in the Southeast. But why a change in projectile point form?

The answer to this question probably lies in hunting techniques. Dr. Joseph Caldwell (see Chapter 1) noted several years ago that "hunting in the forest had to be learned . . . it is quite a different affair from hunting in plains or savannah" (Caldwell 1974:13). He further noted that "the most effective point for the weapon would evidently be one with pronounced barbs or shoulders, to maintain the javelin in the wound and so impede the flight of game" (ibid.). The lanceolate, fluted points are generally seen as representing an adaptation to a plains or grasslands situation where the large Pleistocene mammals were attacked at close quarters. Such a weapon could be imbedded in the quarry, withdrawn, and imbedded again. But with the disappearance of the large game animals and the re-appearance of the dense deciduous forest, new hunting methods were required. Hence, the appearance of a projectile point

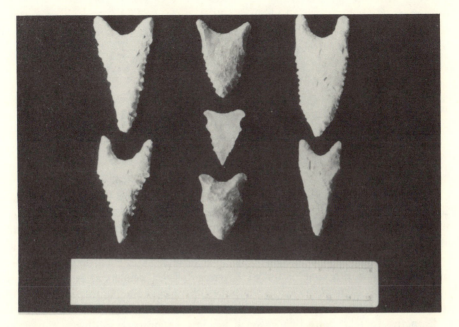

Projectile points associated with the Transitional Phase. Top row (from left): Terrell County, Oconee County (2), and Calhoun County; bottom row: Calhoun County, Gordon County, Terrell County. *(From a private collection)* Photo No. 10

designed to stay in the quarry, as Caldwell has noted. There is no evidence for the use of the bow and arrow at this early time, so it is assumed that the atl-atl, or throwing-stick, was used for launching javelins tipped with stone or bone points (see photo, page 54). That these projectile point types (Dalton, Quad, Hardaway, etc.) followed the fluted points in time has been demonstrated by excavations at a number of sites throughout the Southeast (see Willey *op. cit.*; Mason *op. cit.*; Williams and Stoltman 1965:678; et al.).

Williams and Stoltman suggest that "with the depletion of herds of big game, new sources of food were sought, or more likely, old supplementary subsistence patterns were intensified in favorable localities" *(ibid.)*. Evidence of this intensification (or diversification) is seen at a number of sites dating to the Transitional Phase. Regarding the Quad site in northern Alabama, Walthall (1980:33) notes that the "wide variety of tools from the Quad site indicates that this locality was used as a base camp by hunting and gathering groups." Basically, the same can be said for the earliest level at the Hardaway site in North Carolina (see Coe 1964:64-81), a level dated at about 8,000 B.C. Artifacts from a natural spring in Florida, attributed by the authors to the Paleo-Indian period (see Clausen et al.:1979), indicate a wide range of subsistence techniques. The base of an oak mortar from this site probably indicates utilization of seeds or nuts. However, the dates given would seem to place these artifacts in a slightly later period—the Early Archaic. Recently, most of the dates attributed in the literature to the Transitional Phase have been seriously questioned as being much too late. Dates from a site in Missouri, where Dalton points were found in a pure, undisturbed situation, seem to verify an age of about 8,500 B.C. (Dr. Albert C. Goodyear, personal communication). This would certainly make more sense in light of the environmental occurrences discussed above.

Summary

It has been demonstrated in this chapter that the earliest human inhabitants of Georgia encountered a very different environment from that familiar to us today. Indeed, there is no modern counterpart, for animals associated with more tropical areas lived alongside those typically found in a sub-Arctic or boreal environment, not to mention species of animals now extinct. The forests, too, were different from those of today, with spruce and fir forests covering Georgia perhaps as far south as the northernmost coastal plain. Georgia's earliest peoples were hunters and gatherers, probably depending on the large game animals for most of their needs. They possessed a distinctive tool kit consisting of small scrapers, choppers, lance-shaped fluted projectile points, and other artifacts. While these artifacts are found in all parts of the state, they are most numerous in the coastal plain. As discussed above, it is believed that the coastal plain would have been rich in animal life, and probably in edible plant foods as well. The lance-shaped projectile points were nearly always made of flint or chert, often non-local materials. This indicates that people may have traveled fairly extensively at this time, probably following game, and trade in superior types of flint probably occurred as well. This is not to infer that the Paleo-Indians wandered around aimlessly, for modern hunter-gatherers practice what anthropologists call "restricted wandering." In this, the group, composed of up to fifty people, wanders widely following game animals and collecting food, but staying within a geographic area which is recognized by them and by other groups as representing their territory.

This way of life changed rather abruptly between ca. 10,000 B.C. and ca. 8,000 B.C. as a direct result of environmental change. As the climate became warmer, the coniferous forests retreated northward, and along with them several animal species as well. Perhaps more importantly, the large game animals became scarce or extinct almost everywhere. The re-appearance of the dense, deciduous forest prompted cultural change, a change reflected in projectile point forms. The fluted points had almost certainly represented an adaptation to hunting large game in a grasslands or parkland environment, but with the return of the forest, and with deer as the primary quarry, a new hunting method was required. Thus, the projectile point forms of the Transitional Phase are barbed or shouldered, apparently being designed to stay in the prey. A point made in this fashion would slow the animal's movements and increase blood loss, and thereby increase the hunter's chances of recovering the animal. Other cultural changes, including an increasing use of plant foods and smaller game animals, are evident. These developments laid the foundations for the subsistence pattern typical of the Archaic period, and what Caldwell refers to as "Primary Forest Efficiency."

REFERENCES: CHAPTER III

Anonymous, "New Discoveries," in *Early Man,* Summer, 1979, p. 1.

Blair, W. Frank, "Distributional Patterns of Vertebrates in the Southern United States in Relation to Past and Present Environments," in *Zoogeography,* ed. by Carl L. Hubbs, American Association for the Advancement of Science, Publication No. 51, Washington, D.C., 1958, pp. 433-468.

Butzer, Karl W., *Environment and Archaeology: An Introduction to Pleistocene Geography,* 2nd. ed., Aldine, Atherton, Chicago, 1971.

Caldwell, Joseph R., "The Archaeology of Eastern Georgia and South Carolina," in *Archaeology of the Eastern United States,* ed. by James B. Griffin, University of Chicago Press, 1952, pp. 312-321.

_____, *Trend and Tradition in the Prehistory of the Eastern United States,* Kraus Reprint Co., Millwood, New York, 1974 (reprint of the 1958 edition).

Childers, W. Morlin, and Herbert L. Minshall, "Evidence of Early Man Exposed at Yuha Pinto Wash," *American Antiquity,* Vol. 45, No. 2, 1980, pp. 297-308.

Clausen, C.J., et al., "Little Salt Spring, Florida: A Unique Underwater Site," *Science,* Vol. 203, No. 4381, 1979, pp. 609-14.

Coe, Joffre L., *The Formative Cultures of the Carolina Piedmont,* Transactions of the American Philosophical Society, New Series, Vol. 54, Part 5, 1964.

Davis, Margaret Bryan, "Pleistocene Biogeography of Temperate Deciduous Forests," *Geoscience and Man,* Vol. 13, 1976, pp. 13-26.

Delcourt, Paul A., and Hazel R. Delcourt, "Late Pleistocene and Holocene Distributional History of the Deciduous Forest in the Southeastern United States," in *Contributions to the Knowledge of the Flora and Vegetation of the Carolinas,* ed. by H. Leith and E. Landolt, Veroffentlichungen des Geobotanschen Institutes der Eidg. Techn. Hochschule, Stiftung Rubel, in Zurich, Vol. 1, 1979, pp. 79-107.

_____, "Goshen Springs: Late Quaternary Vegetation Record for Southern Alabama," *Ecology,* Vol. 61, No. 2, 1980, pp. 371-386.

Dragoo, Christine W., "The Proboscidians and Man," *The Archaeology of Eastern North America,* Vol. 7, No. 1, 1979, pp. 180-213.

Fairbanks, Charles H., "Creek and Pre-Creek," in *Archaeology of the Eastern United States,* ed. by James B. Griffin, University of Chicago Press, 1952, pp. 285-300.

Fish, Paul R., *Patterns of Prehistoric Site Distribution in Effingham and Screven Counties, Georgia,* University of Georgia Laboratory of Archaeology Series, Report No. 11, Athens, 1976.

_____, and Suzanne K. Fish, *Prehistoric Settlement in the Dry Creek Watershed,* University of Georgia Laboratory of Archaeology Series, Report No. 14, Athens, 1977.

Flint, Richard Foster, *Glacial and Quaternary Geology,* John Wiley & Sons, New York, 1971.

Frison, George C., and George M. Zeimens, "Bone Projectile Points: An addition to the Folsom Cultural Complex," *American Antiquity,* Vol. 45, No. 2, 1980, pp. 231-237.

Gorman, Frederick, "The Clovis Hunters: An Alternate View of their Environment and Ecology," in *Contemporary Archaeology,* ed. by Mark P. Leone, Southern Illinois University Press, Carbondale, 1972, pp. 206-221.

Haag, William G., "The Bering Strait Land Bridge," in *Early Man in America,* W.H. Freeman and Co., San Francisco, 1973.

Haynes, C. Vance, Jr., "Elephant-Hunting in North America," in *Early Man In America,* W.H. Freeman and Co., San Francisco, 1973, pp. 44-52.

Kelly, A.R., *A Preliminary Report on Archaeological Explorations at Macon, Georgia,* Bureau of American Ethnology, Bulletin 119, Anthropological Papers No. 1, U.S. Government Printing Office, Washington, 1938.

——————————, "An Early Flint Industry in Southwest Georgia," in *Short Contributions to the Geology, Geography, and Archaeology of Georgia,* The Geological Survey Bulletin, No. 56, Department of Mines, Mining, and Geology, State Division of Conservation, Atlanta, pp. 146-153.

Lipps, Lewis, and Clayton E. Ray, "The Pleistocene Fossiliferous Deposit at Ladds, Bartow County, Georgia," *Bulletin of the Georgia Academy of Science,* Vol. 25, No. 3, 1967, pp. 113-119.

Lively, Matthew, "The Lively Complex: Announcing a Pebble Tool Industry in Alabama," *Journal of Alabama Archaeology,* Vol. 11, No. 2, 1965, pp. 103-122.

Martin, Paul S., and John E. Guilday, "A Bestiary for Pleistocene Biologists," in *Pleistocene Extinctions: The Search for a Cause,* ed. by Paul S. Martin and H.W. Wright, Proceedings of the VII Congress of the International Association for Quarternary Research, Yale University Press, New Haven, 1967, pp. 1-62.

——————————, and H.E. Wright, eds., *Pleistocene Extinctions: Search for a Cause,* Proceedings of the VII Congress of the International Association for Quaterny Research, Yale University Press, New Haven, 1967.

Martin, Robert A., and S. David Webb, "Late Pleistocene Mammals from the Devil's Den Fauna, Levy County," in *Pleistocene Mammals of Florida,* ed. by S. David Webb, University of Florida Press, Gainesville, 1974, pp. 114-145.

Mason, Ronald J., "The Paleo-Indian Tradition in Eastern North America," *Current Anthropology,* Vol. 3, No. 3, 1962, pp. 227-278.

Matthews, L. Harrison, *The Life of Mammals, Vol. 2,* Universe Books, New York, 1971.

Michie, James L., "The Late Pleistocene Human Occupation of South Carolina," Unpublished Senior Thesis, Department of Anthropology, University of South Carolina, Columbia, 1977.

Miller, Carl F., "Early Cultural Horizons in the Southeastern United States," *American Antiquity,* Vol. 15, No. 4, 1950, pp. 273-288.

O'Steen, Lisa D., R. Jerald Ledbetter, and Daniel T. Elliott, "PaleoIndian Sites of the Inner Piedmont of Georgia and South Carolina," Paper presented at the Southeastern Archaeological Conference, Columbia, S.C., 1983.

Patterson, Mrs. Wayne, "Notes on the Exploration of the Bull Creek Site, Columbus, Georgia," *Early Georgia,* Vol. 1, No. 1, 1950, pp. 35-40.

Ray, Clayton E., "Pleistocene Mammals from Ladds, Bartow County, Georgia," *Bulletin of the Georgia Academy of Science,* Vol. 25, No. 3, 1967.

Shelford, Victor E., *The Ecology of North America,* University of Illinois Press, Urbana, 1963.

Swanton, John R., *The Indians of the Southeastern United States,* Bureau of American Ethnology, Bulletin 137, U.S. Government Printing Office, Washington, 1946.

Voorhies, M.R., "The Watkins Quarry: A New Late Pleistocene Mammal Locality in Glynn County, Georgia," *Bulletin of the Georgia Academy of Science,* Vol. 29, No. 2, 1971.

——————————, "Pleistocene Vertebrates with Boreal Affinities in the Georgia Piedmont," *Quaternary Research,* Vol. 4, 1974, pp. 85-93.

Waller, Ben I., "Some Occurrences of Paleo-Indian Projectile Points in Florida Waters," *Florida Anthropologist,* Vol. 23, No. 4, 1970, pp. 129-134.

——————————, and James Dunbar, "Distribution of Paleo-Indian Projectiles in Florida," *Florida Anthropologist,* Vol. 30, No. 2, 1977, pp. 79-80.

Walthall, John A., *Prehistoric Indians of the Southeast: Archaeology of Alabama and the Middle South,* University of Alabama Press, University, 1980.

Watts, W.A., "The Full-Glacial Vegetation of Northwestern Georgia," *Ecology,* Vol. 51, No. 1, 1970, pp. 17-33.

——————————, "The Vegetation Record of a Mid-Wisconsin Interstadial in Northwest Georgia," *Quaternary Research,* Vol. 3, 1973, pp. 257-268.

——————————, "Vegetation Record for the Last 20,000 Years from a Small Marsh on Lookout Mountain, Northwestern Georgia," *Geological Society of America Bulletin,* Vol. 86, No. 3, 1975, pp. 287-291.

————————————————, "Late Quaternary Vegetation History at White Pond on the Inner Coastal Plain of South Carolina," *Quaternary Research,* Vo. 13, No. 2, 1980, pp. 187-199.

Wauchope, Robert, *Archaeological Survey of Northern Georgia, With a Test of Some Cultural Hypotheses,* Memoirs of the Society for American Archaeology, No. 21, 1966.

Wetmore, Alexander, "Pleistocene *Aves* from Ladds, Georgia," *Bulletin of the Georgia Academy of Science,* Vol. 25, No. 3, 1967, pp. 151-153.

Whitehead, Donald R., "Studies of Full-Glacial Vegetation and Climate in Southeastern United States," in *Quaternary Paleoecology,* ed. by E.J. Cushing and H.E. Wright, Jr., Yale University Press, New Haven, 1967, pp. 237-248.

Willey, Gordon R., *An Introduction to American Archaeology, Vol. 1: North and Middle America,* Prentice-Hall, Inc., Englewood Cliffs, New Jersey, 1966.

Williams, Stephen, ed., *The Waring Papers: The Southern Cult, and Other Archaeological Essays,* University of Georgia Press, Athens, 1965a.

————————————————, ed., *Proceedings of the 20th Southeastern Archaeological Conference,* Bulletin No. 2, 1965b.

————————————————, and James B. Stoltman, "An Outline of Southeastern United States Prehistory with Partucular Emphasis on the Paleo-Indian Era," in *The Quaternary of the United States,* ed. by H.E. Wright and David G. Frey, Princeton University Press, Princeton, New Jersey, 1965, pp. 669-683.

Wormington, H.M., *Ancient Man in North America,* Denver Museum of Natural History, Popular Series No. 4, Denver, 1957.

Chapter IV

THE ARCHAIC PERIOD
The Early Archaic (Ca. 8000–5000 B.C.)

Several years ago, the late Joseph R. Caldwell noted the incomplete dependence on agriculture witnessed among the historic tribes of Georgia (Caldwell 1958:12). Indeed, those tribes living along the coast were seen as having been only marginally agricultural. Hunting, fishing, and gathering activities formed major sources of food, and while those tribes living in the interior portions of Georgia were more dependent on agriculture, they also derived a substantial amount of their food from hunting, fishing, and gathering. Caldwell believed that this subsistence pattern represented a successful means of exploiting local food sources which had been established millenia before and which had proven so efficient that it was retained, at least in part, even after agriculture appeared. This early pattern of hunting, gathering, and fishing is what he referred to as "primary forest efficiency." This adaptation was viewed as evidence of man's success in adjusting to new environmental conditions following the final glacial episode some 12,000 years ago. The new life-way marks the beginning of the Archaic, a time period spanning some 7,000 years in Georgia prehistory.

The Archaic period is generally thought to have begun with the "settling in" process, the completion of adjustment to the new environmental situation brought on by the return of the deciduous forest over much of the eastern United States. A pattern of seasonal exploitation of local resources emerged, a pattern which may differ from one region to another. As Willey (1966:60) notes, traits associated with the Archaic "reflect a variety of regional adaptations." Thus, those groups living in coastal areas would have exploited food sources different from those of groups living in inland areas. Peoples living in the mountains and Piedmont would have had patterns of exploitation different in some ways from those of groups living in the Coastal Plain. In most areas, there is evidence of a pattern of movements based on the utilization of food sources available on a seasonal basis. A group or band of people might, for instance, return to the same upland campsite year after year to collect acorns and other nuts and to hunt during autumn. In the winter and spring months, they would live at another location where perhaps other types of food could be obtained. In summer, they might move to still another location to fish, pick berries, etc. Artifacts recovered at such campsites can give important clues as to the type of campsite represented and the kinds of subsistence activities carried out at that location.

Artifacts made of perishable materials, such as wood, fiber, basketry, leather, etc. are rarely preserved in the archaeological record in the Southeast. Accordingly, most of the artifacts by which archaeologists interpret the past in this area are made of stone, bone, or pottery. For the Archaic period, stone projectile points, knives, and scrapers are among the artifacts most commonly found. Projectile points in particular are important, for certain forms prevailed at different times. The excavation of a few deeply stratified sites in Georgia and other southeastern states has enabled archaeologists to construct a sequence of projectile point types for the Archaic. Sometimes, there are carbon dates which give us some idea of the time period during which specific types were most popular. The major types of projectile points will be presented below, but to avoid confusion, nomenclature will be kept to a minimum.

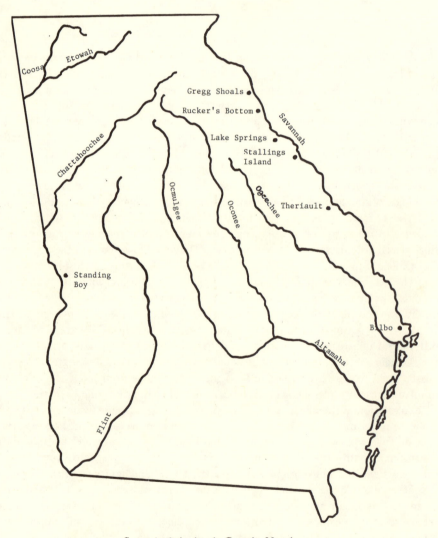

Some Archaic sites in Georgia. Map 4.

Archaeologists are all too fond of giving a separate name for each projectile point exhibiting some minor variation, and thus there are literally hundreds of named projectile points. Many were contemporary, and indeed some from an individual site or nearby sites may even have been made by the same individual.

Following the Dalton, Quad, and other projectile point forms associated with the Transitional period, there appeared projectile points which were corner-notched and often beveled. Among the earliest of these is the Palmer corner-notched type described by Coe (1964:67) as a small, corner-notched projectile point exhibiting basal grinding and serrated edges. Carbon dates from a site in east Tennessee indicate that the Palmer points date from about 7500 B.C. (see Chapman 1976). They were found in the layer immediately above the Dalton level at a site in the North Carolina Piedmont and the Cal Smoak site in the South Carolina Coastal Plain yielded Palmer points from a layer tentatively dated to about 7000 B.C. (Anderson et al. 1979). Palmer points are found throughout Georgia as surface finds, but recently they have been found *in situ* in two stratified sites along the Savannah River. At the deeply stratified Gregg Shoals site, Palmer points were found in an early Archaic context (Tippitt and Marquardt 1984) and at the Rucker's Bottom site several Palmer points were found along with numerous other artifacts typical of early Archaic assemblages elsewhere (Anderson and Schuldenrein 1983). Many of the Palmer points from these two sites are made of non-local material, generally thought to have been obtained from quarries to the south.

In eastern Georgia, one of the earliest Archaic projectile point types is the Taylor point. Described by Michie (1966:123) as a beveled, side-notched point having a concave base and exhibiting basal grinding, it was found in the deepest levels at the im-

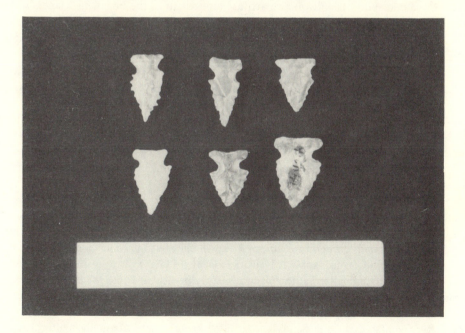

Early Archaic projectile points (Palmer) from northwest Georgia. *(From a private collection)* Photo No. 11

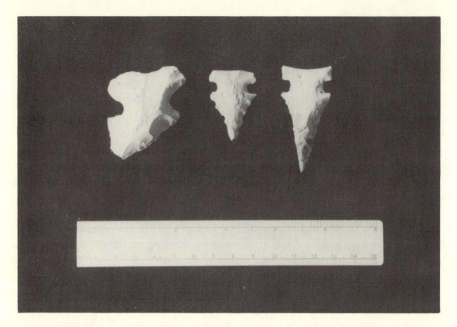

Edgefield scraper and associated projectile point types (Taylor). (Left to right: Burke County, northwest Georgia, Calhoun County.) *(From a private collection)* Photo No. 12

portant Theriault site in Burke County (see Brockington 1971). Apparently associated with the Taylor point is a distinctive artifact referred to as the Edgefield scraper (see Michie 1972). Described as a hafted scraper with wide, deep side notches and a working edge located at an angle of approximately forty-five degrees to the medial axis, it was found in association with the Taylor points at the Theriault site. This artifact type occurs primarily in the Coastal Plain of Florida, Georgia, and South Carolina, with occasional specimens being recorded from the Piedmont. Most Edgefield scrapers are made from Coastal Plains chert, which occurs in a belt from Tampa, Florida, to the Savannah River (Goodyear et al. 1980:4). Even those specimens reported from the Piedmont are usually made from this marine chert. In Georgia, the northernmost example known of the Edgefield scraper is one reported from Banks County, on the northern edge of the Piedmont (see White 1982). It, too, is made from Coastal Plains chert.

In Georgia and surrounding areas, a variety of other corner-notched projectile points belonging to the early Archaic is mentioned in the archaeological literature. In Alabama, Cambron and Waters (1959:79, 83) discovered that at the Flint Creek rock shelter a small, corner-notched point was in the stratum immediately overlying the zone containing Quad points (Transitional Paleo-Indian). They named this type the Decatur point and note that the blade is sharply beveled and that the base has been thinned by flaking, producing a slight incurvature. The flat basal edges and the notches exhibit evidence of grinding. In the Tennessee Valley area of northern Alabama, projectile points of the Big Sandy type follow Dalton materials in the cultural sequence. Big Sandy points are described as being side-notched and exhibiting triangular blades and serrated blade edges. Grinding has usually been done in the hafting area and some specimens are beveled, possibly because of re-sharpening (Walthall 1980:49). Because these points are found primarily where most of the Dalton points are found in Alabama, and because of the similarity of associated artifacts, Walthall (*op. cit.*:50) suggests strong cultural continuity, i.e., Big Sandy point types developed out of the earlier Dalton types. Also like Dalton points they have been found in both open-air sites and in rock shelters. Although Big Sandy points are found in other states from Florida to the Great Lakes, nowhere do they appear in great numbers (*ibid.*). Both Decatur and Big Sandy points are found in Georgia.

In southwestern Georgia, the Standing Boy flint industry has been described as containing projectile points analogous to the Decatur and other corner-notched varieties (see Huscher 1964). These points are described as being beveled and notched, and they exhibit advanced patination. Kellar and McMichael (1960:203) speculate that the Standing Boy artifacts may have developed out of Paleo-Indian industries in this part of the state, and DePratter (1975:9) suggests that this industry may represent the earliest Archaic cultures in southwest Georgia.

Thus, throughout Georgia and the Southeast, projectile points associated with the Transitional Period were replaced by corner-notched or side-notched points, with scrapers and other tools remaining virtually the same. Slight variations from one region to another have given rise to separate names for many of these points, which

Various types of scrapers associated with Early Archaic or Transitional Paleo-Indian (Dalton) cultures. (Specimen in lower right corner is an Edgefield scraper. All are from Banks County.) *(From a private collection)* Photo No. 13

are more or less contemporary and all are believed to have been developed out of the earlier point styles by peoples in each area. While some of these point types are widespread, others, such as the Taylor point and the associated Edgefield scraper, seem to be less widely distributed.

Following the Palmer and related projectile point types in the early Archaic sequence are types identified by archaeologists as Kirk points. Kirk points are of three types: corner-notched, stemmed, and serrated (see Coe 1964:69, 70). The corner-notched variety is described as a large triangular blade with a straight base, corner notches, and serrated edges. The blade is larger than that of the Palmer points and is sometimes beveled. The Kirk stemmed type has a long dagger-like blade with deep serrations and a broad stem, while the Kirk serrated point has a long narrow blade with deep serrations and a broad, square stem. At sites in east Tennessee, Chapman (1976:2) obtained carbon dates from material found in association with Kirk corner-notched varieties indicating their use during the period 7500-6900 B.C. In the North Carolina Piedmont, they were found in the midden overlying the Palmer types at the Hardaway site (Coe *op. cit.*). In West Virginia, materials associated with Kirk points at the St. Albans site yielded a carbon date of 6980 B.C. (Broyles 1971:63). As with the other varieties discussed, Kirk-type projectile points are found widely in Georgia. They were represented in the collections from the survey of the Richard B. Russell reservoir on the upper Savannah River (Taylor and Smith 1978:317; Tippett and Marquardt 1984) and were present in the earliest level at the Boas site in Floyd County, northwest Georgia, excavated by a team from Shorter College (Warner 1974). Kirk types are also to be seen in the north Georgia collection made by Wauchope (1966).

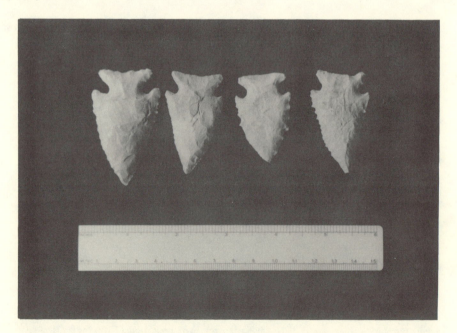

Early Archaic (Kirk) projectile points. (Smallest specimen is from Murray County; others are from Dade County.) *(From a private collection)* **Photo No. 14**

The final early Archaic point type to be considered is the bifurcate-stemmed type or types. These points are small and have indented, bifurcate stems. The blade edges are usually serrated. Since many of the later Kirk forms have indented bases and serrated edges, it has been suggested that the bifurcate-stemmed style developed out of Kirk forms (see Walthall *op. cit.*:54). At the St. Albans site in Kanawha County, West Virginia, the side-notched bifurcate-stemmed points were dated to approximately 6700 B.C., and the LeCroy bifurcate-stemmed variety was dated at 6300 B.C. (Broyles 1971). At Rose Island and other sites in east Tennessee, Chapman (1976) obtained dates of 6770 B.C. for the side-notched bifurcate-stemmed points and 6300 B.C. for the LeCroy points.

Bifurcate-stemmed points are known from several locations in Georgia. They are represented in the Mell collection, a private collection curated at the University of Georgia and composed of artifacts from sites in and around Clarke County. Bifurcate-stemmed points are represented in the collections from the Richard B. Russell reservoir survey (Taylor and Smith *op. cit.*) and were found on a site in Clayton County (DePratter 1975:11). Such points can be seen in private collections from northeast Georgia, although nowhere are they common.

From the foregoing discussion, one might get the idea that projectile points are virtually the only artifact type recovered from Archaic sites. While they do form a major artifact category, there are other artifacts which are common on sites of this time period. Among them are stone scrapers of several types, stone knives, perforators, drills, choppers, bone awls, antler-tip projectile points, antler flaking tools, and hammerstones. In levels associated with Kirk projectile point types at Russell Cave in northeastern Alabama, stone mortars and pestles were found (Walthall 1980:54).

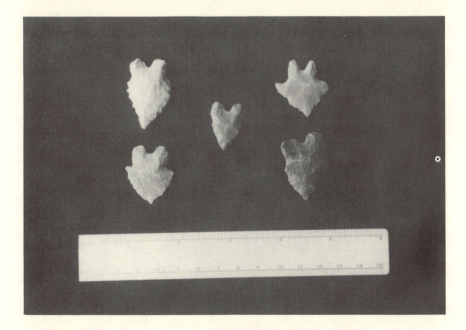

Bifurcate-stemmed projectile points (northwest Georgia). *(From a private collection)* Photo No. 15

Antler-tip projectile points (socketed). *(Jenkins County; from a private collection)*
Photo No. 16

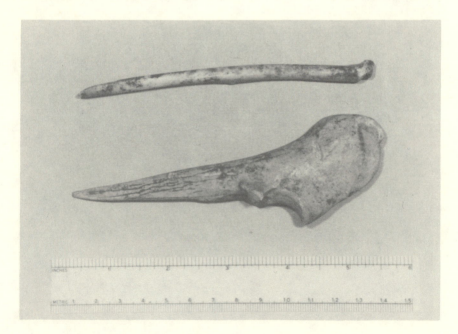

Bone awls from an Archaic site in Georgia. *(Union County; from a private collection)*
Photo No. 17

This, of course, strongly suggests the utilization of plant foods, probably nuts. In east Tennessee, grinding stones were found in Kirk levels at Rose Island and the Icehouse Bottom site, along with charred acorn and hickory nut remains (*ibid.*). Interestingly, the base of what has been identified as a carved oak mortar was recovered from the Little Salt Spring in Florida and has been carbon dated at 9080 B.P. (Clausen et al. 1979:611). This has tremendous implications in that wooden mortars apparently were being used at an early time and therefore the absence of stone mortars on a site should not necessarily be interpreted as indicating a lack of utilization of nuts or other plant foods. As was mentioned earlier in this chapter, wooden artifacts are rarely preserved in the archaeological record and the Florida find is certainly unique. Finally, a wide range of bone and antler tools was found associated with Kirk points at Russell Cave.

Summary of the Early Archaic

Several factors must be brought out relative to our understanding of the early Archaic in Georgia. First of all, few sites from this time period have actually been excavated in Georgia, and some that have were never reported in the form of published works. Apparently few if any records exist on some other sites, as for example the Dairy Field site, briefly mentioned in Caldwell (1958). Thus, it is requisite to turn to sites in surrounding states for which more adequate records exist. It is reasonable to assume that peoples living in the same or similar geographic and environmental circumstances, and often separated by less than one hundred miles would be exploiting their environment in much the same fashion. Thus, we refer to sites dating to the early Archaic in Alabama, Florida, South Carolina, North Carolina, and Tennessee. Artifacts found in surface collections in Georgia are identical to those described from excavated sites in the above states, indicating that people in Georgia shared the artifact types and styles found among peoples in neighboring states, and presumably their life style as well.

Some of these sites were excavated before recovery techniques were refined. Thus, valuable sources of data are now lost. Specifically, the flotation technique now enables archaeologists to recover plant seeds, tiny bones, and other indicators of the diet of prehistoric peoples (Schnieder 1973). Flotation was discovered in the early 1960's, and sites excavated prior to its adoption as a field technique lack this crucial data (Struever 1964). The remains mentioned above are recovered by running water over a bucket- or tubfull of dirt scraped from a house site, cooking pit, trash pit, or other archaeological feature. The bottom of the bucket or tub has been previously removed and replaced by a fine-mesh screen, which traps tiny artifacts which would not be detected by other methods. This is why flotation is now such an important part of archaeological field techniques.

Finally, the vagaries of preservation must not be omitted. Some soils are highly acid, lessening the chances for bone to be preserved. Furthermore, predators (foxes, dogs, wolves, etc.) probably destroyed much of the garbage around Indian campsites, thus removing it from the archaeological record. Tubers, roots, and green plants, all known to have been dietary elements of historic tribes of the area, are not preserved at all in the archaeological record (except in extremely unusual circumstances, such as dry caves, where dried plant remains and roots have been found). Basically, the only plant remains from early Archaic contexts are charred nut remains and some seeds, most recovered after flotation was introduced.

Nevertheless, the evidence at hand suggests that peoples living in what is now Georgia and the Southeast adapted in similar ways to changing environmental conditions at the close of the final glaciation. It is believed that Paleo-Indians adapted by changing their hunting techniques, this change being reflected in the tool assemblages associated with the Transitional Phase. The completion of this adjustment resulted in the establishment of a yearly round of subsistence activities based upon the exploitation of seasonal resources. The "settling in" process, the adjusting of cultures to the local environment, marks the beginning of the Archaic Period. While projectile points in the early Archaic are generally believed to have been developed out of the Dalton and other Transitional Phase forms, there is a high degree of carry-over of other tool types. As an example, the Big Sandy horizon in northern Alabama contains in addition to Big Sandy points, uniface scrapers, biface scrapers, side-scrapers, uniface and biface knives, all of which are also found in the Dalton occupation of the area (Tuck 1974: 75). Continuity is therefore demonstrated between the two traditions. The same carry-over is believed to have occurred in other areas as well.

At the important Stanfield-Worley Bluff Shelter in northern Alabama, the Dalton/ Big Sandy levels yielded a large amount of animal bone, primarily deer. This is in keeping with other Dalton levels where bone is preserved and which are described in the literature. Archaeologists interpret this as representing the replacement of the now extinct Pleistocene megafauna by the deer as the primary quarry of hunters. However, other animal remains were also found in this level at the Stanfield-Worley site and are indicative of the wide range of species being exploited by early Archaic hunters. They include raccoon, rabbit, squirrel, gray fox, chipmunk, porcupine, turkey, bobwhite, and turtle (Walthall 1980:48). Since no plant processing tools were found, it is suggested that this may have been a winter hunting camp.

Further indication of the variety of animals exploited by early Archaic peoples is seen in remains recovered from the Kirk level at Russell Cave in northwestern Alabama. Found here were the remains of 20 turkeys, 155 squirrels, 8 deer, 5 raccoons, 3 skunks, 4 porcupines, 1 bobcat, and a now extinct form of peccary. In all, 18 species of mammals and 10 species of birds were represented in the faunal sample, leading Walthall (op. cit.:54) to conclude that these people excelled in hunting and trapping. A wide range of bone and antler tools, including awls and needles, were also recovered from this level.

Excluding the elusive plant remains, what we have is an indication of an unspecialized economy based upon eating almost all species of birds and mammals. This is precisely the situation reflected at the Modoc Rock Shelter in Illinois for the same time period, i.e., a time when Archaic peoples were learning about the woodland environment, were learning to hunt, trap, and gather a wide range of foodstuffs, and apparently were not very dependent upon any one food source (see Fowler 1959). As the Archaic progressed, however, this situation changed. Some food sources did become much more important than others and a more pronounced seasonal round of subsistence activities came into being, a pattern based upon exploiting a relatively few, dependable resources. This narrowing of the spectrum heralds the next phase, the middle Archaic.

Middle Archaic (5000-2500 B.C.)

Climatic events which played such an important role in cultural events in the Southeast in earlier times now come into play again. The beginning of the middle Archaic can be correlated with the onset of the Altithermal, a time when the climate in the Southeast was warmer and drier than at present. This warming and drying trend began about 5000 B.C. and is believed to have ended about 2500 B.C. One result was that rivers throughout the area became lower and more sluggish because of the decreased rainfall. On the larger streams, and especially around shoals, freshwater mussels abounded, and because of the lower water level, they were now accessible to the people of the area. Apparently, the subsistence patterns of people living near the larger rivers were altered to include this abundant, and hitherto inaccessible, resource.

The middle Archaic is not well-known anywhere in the Southeast, but the change in subsistence patterns is reflected in artifacts recovered from a number of sites in states bordering Georgia. An example is the Eva site in west-central Tennessee. At this site, archaeologists found that mussel shells were scarce in the lower levels, but increased as time went on. At the height of the Altithermal, the Three Mile phase (4000-2000 B.C.) yields evidence for major dependence on riverine food sources. Although the stratum left by the people at this time is some three feet thick, nowhere is there evidence of flooding. This is further indication of drier conditions and a lower water level in the streams. It was in this cultural stratum (the Three Mile phase) that the use of shellfish, fish, and birds vastly increased, for there is a massive deposit of shells (see Lewis and Lewis 1961). While there was abundant animal bone in the earlier Eva component, it is much scarcer in the Three Mile component, a situation which leads the authors to surmise that the much drier conditions had witnessed upland forests giving way to prairies in this part of Tennessee. Thus, the numbers of deer and other animal populations dependent upon mast and browse declined. The earlier Eva level had contained a mortar, pestle, and nutstone, objects also found in the Three Mile component and indicative of the use of nuts as dietary supplements. Also, fish hooks were rare in the earlier level, but common in the Three Mile deposit (*op. cit.*:81). The Eva projectile point types, associated with this site, apparently have a very limited distribution and are not known to be represented in Georgia.

In the North Carolina Piedmont, Coe (*op. cit.*) found the middle Archaic sequence beginning with projectile points he refers to as the Stanly type. This point is described as having a broad triangular blade with a small squared stem and a shallow-notched base. This point type was the earliest projectile point at the Doerschuk site and was found associated with a semi-lunar shaped atl-atl weight, stone drills, scrapers, quarry blades, hammerstones, a mortar, and numerous fragments of chipped and worked stone (Coe *op. cit.*:35, 54). These points were followed by a type Coe named Morrow Mountain. He distinguished between two types: Morrow Mountain I, characterized by a small triangular blade with a short, pointed stem; and Morrow Mountain II, which has a long, narrow blade and a long, tapered stem (*op. cit.*:37).

Morrow Mountain projectile points. *(Towns County; from a private collection)* **Photo No. 18**

The final middle Archaic projectile point described by Coe for the North Carolina Piedmont is the Guilford point. Described as a long, slender but thick blade with a straight, rounded, or concave base, it followed the Morrow Mountain types in the cultural sequence, and was found associated with a chipped stone ax (*op. cit.*:43). Carbon dates presented by Coe for this level at the Gaston site indicate a date of about 4000 B.C. for the Guilford point, and on this basis he assigns the date of 4500 B.C. for the earliest Morrow Mountain level. Dates from Morrow Mountain levels at sites in Alabama closely agree (Walthall 1980:60-61), although one date from east Tennessee is as early as about 5000 B.C. (Chapman 1976:8).

Stanly, Morrow Mountain, and Guilford projectile point types are all found in Georgia, especially in the Piedmont and northward. Morrow Mountain points were found in a level overlying early Archaic artifacts at the Rucker's Bottom site in Elbert County (Anderson and Schuldernrein 1981:14). These were almost all made of quartz, a trait noticed earlier in this same region by Taylor and Smith (1978:321). Middle Archaic points are frequently represented in surface collections from the Piedmont of Georgia, but there are comparatively few excavations where they are found in sequence. One excavation which did yield a Morrow Mountain point, but no carbon date, was at the Griffin Site in Floyd County, excavated by a team from Shorter College (Warner 1974). Both Morrow Mountain and Stanley points were found in excavations in the Ocmulgee Bottoms and at the Lake Springs site near Augusta. Middle Archaic artifacts were well-represented in the collections resulting from a survey in Monroe County (Fish et al.:1978:1). It is during the middle Archaic that the semi-lunar shaped atl-atl weight is believed to have appeared in the cultural assemblage in Georgia, as it did in North Carolina and elsewhere (see photo 22 on page 57).

50

In Alabama, the middle Archaic saw the appearance and diffusion of new types of artifacts, including ground stone tools and bone or antler implements (Walthall *op. cit.*: 59). Several projectile point types identified with the middle Archaic in other states are also present in Alabama. One site yielded a Morrow Mountain point associated with a hearth which was carbon dated to 4500 B.C. (*op. cit.*:60). In one rockshelter, Morrow Mountain points were associated with pitted nutting stones, grinding stones, and manos. Burials from the middle Archaic (Morrow Mountain) level at Russell Cave in northeastern Alabama yielded dates of 4300 B.C. All the individuals had been interred in a flexed position and the teeth of the adults were heavily worn, suggesting a coarse, gritty diet (Walthall *op. cit.*:61). Morrow Mountain burials at the Stanfield-Worley site included an antler atl-atl hook, an artifact also found in burials at the Eva site in Tennessee. It is believed that the Morrow Mountain peoples were among the earliest inhabitants of the great shell mounds along the Tennessee River (p. 62).

Before going further, it is necessary to discuss an apparently middle Archaic manifestation in the Piedmont of Georgia and South Carolina. This is what Caldwell (1954) referred to as the "Old Quartz Industry." His concept was based upon the discovery of artifacts approximately six feet below the surface and three to four feet beneath late Archaic deposits at the Lake Spring site in Columbia County, Georgia. He noted that these artifacts were very similar to surface finds from at least fifty sites in the northeastern Piedmont of Georgia and in western South Carolina. He described the artifacts as follows:

"The usual surface collections comprise a handful or more of quartz artifacts, chips, and infrequent specimens of marine flint. Most frequent artifact types are ovate blades, not core tools, but often small, well made, and finished with secondary chipping. Diminutive oppositely beveled, so called 'spinner points,' together with side and end scrapers form consistent minorities."

(Caldwell 1954:37)

Caldwell (1974:36) went on to note that the oldest sites which he discovered in his survey of the Hartwell reservoir were Old Quartz.

Old Quartz Industry sites are now known to occur widely in the Piedmont of Georgia and adjacent portions of South Carolina. Hundreds of sites containing the characteristic small scatter of quartz artifacts, including ovate points or bifaces, have been located in the Georgia Piedmont in the years since Caldwell identified this assemblage (See DePratter 1975:11). These sites were numerous on hilltops in the Stone Mountain area (Dickens 1964:45), and Old Quartz sites proved to be the most distinctive type in the Trotters Shoals survey in Elbert County (Hutto 1970:33). Such sites were also found to be quite common in Richmond and Columbia Counties and in adjacent Aiken and Edgefield Counties, South Carolina (Neill 1966:1). In this area, however, Old Quartz sites were not found below the Fall Line, but only north of it, where quartz occurs. Sites assigned to the Old Quartz Industry were found in the Oliver Basin, an area of the southwest Piedmont in Georgia, surveyed by McMichael and Kellar (1960).

Earlier, Caldwell believed that the Old Quartz Industry represented a period between the Paleo-Indian and the Archaic periods in the Piedmont (Caldwell 1958:8).

He believed that the site pattern and assemblage of artifacts indicated "forest nomadism," a way of life in which there was little dependence on any one resource. More recent evidence places this industry considerably later, however, and much earlier tool types have been found in the Piedmont since Caldwell's time. One site which indicates the temporal position of the Old Quartz materials was discovered near the Coosawattee River in Murray County. The site was discovered in the course of archaeological excavations during the construction of the dam at Carter's Quarters. Although it was a multicomponent site, it did contain two stratified components of the Old Quartz Industry. The lower level of this site yielded a carbon date of 6430 B.C., thus placing the Old Quartz Industry in northwest Georgia in the latter part of the early Archaic, assuming the date is reliable. Elsewhere, numerous authors have cited the similarity of Caldwell's Old Quartz points to Morrow Mountain points, even going so far as to say that Old Quartz is merely the Piedmont expression of Morrow Mountain.

One of the features often cited about so-called Old Quartz sites is the absence of large tools, such as grinding stones, mortars, and pestles. Because of this, some archaeologists have suggested that Old Quartz sites, consisting of quartz chips and a few quartz projectile points or other tools, represent temporary campsites of a highly nomadic people who were particularly oriented toward the exploitation of food resources found in and near streams and stream valleys (see Dickens 1964:48, Hutto 1970:33; Caldwell 1958:9). Most Old Quartz sites are on hilltops or at the base of valley slopes near streams, thus being in a riverine life zone. Throughout the region, locally obtained quartz was the favored raw material for manufacturing projectile points, and it is not unusual to find sites near quartz outcrops.

The Middle Archaic: A Summary

The Middle Archaic in Georgia and the Southeast can be distinguished by both climatic and cultural events, which were interconnected. Climatically, the Altithermal began at this time (ca. 5000 B.C.) and this period saw a warming and drying trend set in, a pattern which lasted for about 2000 years. As rainfall decreased, the water level in rivers throughout the area dropped so that swift-flowing streams became rather sluggish. This situation apparently opened up a valuable new food source to the human inhabitants of the region—freshwater mussels. These molluscs abounded around the shoals and rapids of the Tennessee, Savannah, and other large streams, and with the lowered water level, they would have been readily accessible to Archaic peoples for the first time.

That the area's prehistoric inhabitants seized upon this opportunity is attested to in the archaeological record. Especially along the Tennessee and Savannah Rivers, shell middens began to form. These middens, composed primarily of mussel shells discarded by prehistoric diners, also contain other artifacts which can reveal to archaeologists a more complete picture of life at the time. Many times, people were buried in these shell heaps and utilitarian objects, such as bone awls, projectile points, etc., were often placed with them. Concerning these shell heaps along the Tennessee River, Webb and DeJarnette say the following:

"The most obvious fact about the shell mounds is that they are on the immediate bank of the river, so near that they are at times subject to erosion by the river and to silting by floods. They are always adjacent to a shoal . . . on which great quantitites of *mollusca* of many species were to be found . . . Not only was there a great variety in the food of this kind, but its never-failing supply encouraged men to live near a certain source. Seemingly, they did not carry the mussels very far from the shoals before using them for food. It may be . . . that the huge amount of shell in any midden has all come from the river in the immediate vicinity . . . . Wherever shoals appeared in the river, there on the bank, often on both sides of the river, and sometimes on islands nearby, shell mounds are to be found."

(Webb and DeJarnette as quoted in Walthall 1980:66)

The exploitation of this new, stable food source evidently meant a shift in economic patterns for those people living in areas near large streams. One result seems to have been increased sedentism, i.e., people lived in one place for a longer period of time and evidently came back to the same spot year after year. Thus, heaps of mollusc shells, discarded after a meal, began to accumulate and still mark these habitual living areas.

New artifact types appearing in the middle Archaic include antler atl-atl hooks, celts and other stone tools which have been smoothed by grinding. Bone tools apparently came to be more widely used than previously, and this may have been the case with projectile points made of antler tips. However, these latter were in use much earlier, as has been demonstrated at the Little Salt Spring site in Florida (Clausen et al. *op. cit.*). Other types of artifacts, including stone netsinkers, nutting stones, grinding stones, and pestles either appear in the archaeological record for the first time, or continued in use from the early Archaic. All indications are that the prehistoric peoples living in Georgia and the rest of the Southeast were becoming much more efficient in exploiting food sources in whatever locale they happened to be. An oak digging-stick, possibly indicating the utilization of edible roots or tubers, was recovered at the Little Salt Spring site in Florida (*op. cit.*) and this along with nutting stones and grinding equipment found in sites elsewhere indicate that nuts, berries, and other types of plant foods were important at this time. In animal remains from middle Archaic sites, there is usually little difference between early and middle Archaic assemblages. At Russel Cave, the middle Archaic levels saw a decrease in the number of squirrel and bird remains, but at sites from Florida to Tennessee, deer, opossum, bear, raccoon, and other small animal remains are common. For those people living near large streams, mussels became important and figured more and more in their economy.

The numerous shell heaps along the rivers mark places where people returned year after year to exploit the nearby molluscs, but in areas away from such major streams, molluscs did not figure prominently, if at all, in the diet of the people. In these areas, probably the seasonal pattern of exploitation of local food sources went on more or less uninterrupted from the early Archaic. However, new types of tools and new styles of projectile points diffused throughout the Southeast. Aside from drier conditions, changes in local environments during the Altithermal probably were not drastic. In the Coastal Plain of South Carolina, a predominately modern pine

Drawing showing how the atl-atl, or throwing-stick was used. *(Courtesy National Park Service, Ocmulgee National Monument)* **Photo No. 19**

forest was established by about 5000 B.C. (Watts 1980:194), and a modern forest is believed to have existed in the Valdosta, Georgia, area by at least 3000 B.C. (Watts 1971:686). We now know that late Archaic peoples used these pine forests and of course those areas forested in hardwoods would have been heavily exploited, not only for their plant foods, but also for the birds and animals which congregated there to feed on the mast. The Plant Scherer survey in Monroe County found that most of the Archaic sites in the area surveyed were located near stream confluences in red soils, which are believed to have supported a mixed hardwood forest (Fish et al. 1978:48).

The working out of a seasonal pattern of movement based on the utilization of certain seasonally available foods apparently led to some specialization in the economy

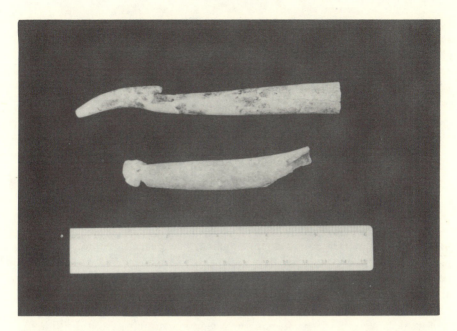

Bone atl-atl hooks (socketed). *(Top specimen is from Tennessee; other is from Stallings Island, near Augusta. From a private collection)* **Photo No. 20**

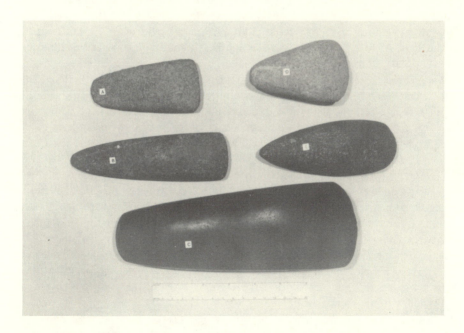

Examples of celts found in Georgia. All have been smoothed by grinding. *(A, Bartow County; B, Gordon County; C, Rabun County; D, Gordon County; E, White County; from a private collection)* **Photo No. 21**

of Archaic peoples. This became much more true for middle Archaic peoples living in areas where freshwater mussels were available. This resource evidently gave rise to increased sedentism. By about 4000 B.C. in north central Florida, people were spending more time along the St. Johns River than in the Uplands, indicating the importance of shellfish in that area (Milanich and Fairbanks 1980:147). A multiplicity of hunting and gathering activities are evidenced in the shell middens along the Tennessee and other inland rivers. The reliability of the shellfish resource, and the sedentism which it apparently gave rise to, ushers in the final stage of this period, the late Archaic.

Late Archaic (2500-1000 B.C.)

The late Archaic was a time when once again the climate began to change, this time to a cooler, wetter, more modern situation. The gradual return of wetter conditions ultimately meant that rivers and streams rose to more or less modern levels and the forest type dominating in each particular region in Georgia was essentially the same as that found by the earliest Europeans to visit the state. As was the case in earlier times, this climatic change stimulated cultural changes. Peoples living along the Savannah and other large streams continued to intensively exploit shellfish, but as the water level rose, it is believed that the shellfish became increasingly inaccessible toward the end of the Archaic period. There is evidence that Archaic peoples also intensively exploited coastal resources during this time, for shell middens appeared along the coast, on the islands, and in and around marshes and tidal creeks. Many innovations in tool types, projectile point forms, and subsistence activities occurred in the Late Archaic in Georgia and the Southeast, and these changes and discoveries will be discussed below.

One of the most widely known late Archaic sites in Georgia is the Stallings Island site. Located on an island in the Savannah River a few miles above Augusta, the site consists of a very large shell mound, described in the 1930's as being 512 feet long, 300 feet wide, and rising to an average height of 23 feet above river level (Claflin 1931). The island was situated just below some rapids prior to construction of the Clark Hill Dam. In past years, portions of the mound had been cultivated, while part was covered in forest growth. C.C. Jones wrote about the site in his monumental work on Georgia prehistory, and records that he dug a few pits in the shell mound, encountering skeletons, beads, pipes, axes, and fragments of pottery (Jones *op. cit.*). In 1929, a team from the Peabody Museum of Harvard University visited the site and conducted exploratory excavations into the mound. Their work demonstrated that the cultural deposit arose on a natural elevation of clay left by the eroding of the Savannah River. This cultural deposit revealed the presence of several types of artifacts, burials, fire-hearths, etc. Among the artifacts were some distinctive types now widely associated with the late Archaic.

Bone artifacts form a distinctive artifact category revealed in the excavation of the Stallings Island mound. The prehistoric people living here made extensive use of bone, mostly the leg bones and antlers of deer. Bone artifacts were found in all stages of manufacture, allowing the archaeologists to establish a rather complete record of how such tools were made. Among those bone tools found were awls, needles, and pins, some of the latter being decorated with carvings. A large number of antler flakers, used in the final stages of manufacturing chipped stone tools, was found. Fewer quantities of bone fish hooks and bone projectile points were encountered.

Among the stone artifacts recovered were banner stones (atl-atl weights), some unfinished grooved axes, grinding stones, mortars, netsinkers, and perforated steatite slabs. Over 2,500 of the latter were found (see photos 31, 32 on pages 65, 66). Thousands of chipped stone artifacts were encountered by the archaeologists working at this site. Many of the artifacts are identifiable as projectile points, presumably for the atl-atl, since they are up to three inches long and thus too heavy for use with a bow and arrow. Among these, the square-stemmed projectile point, now known as the Savannah River point, was particularly common and has come to be accepted as a hallmark of the late Archaic. However, points with rounded rather than square stems were also common (see Claflin *op. cit.*). The perforated steatite (soapstone) slabs were commonly identified as net-sinkers, but Caldwell's excavations in the Allatoona reservoir a few years later (see Chapter 5) strongly indicates their use as boilers in "fire-less cooking." In this, the stones are heated over a fire, then dipped in a waterproof basket or other container, causing the soup or gruel to boil. Furthermore, these artifacts have been found on sites where their use as netsinkers would have been highly improbable.

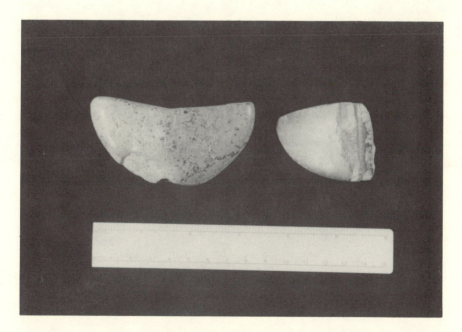

Semi-lunar atl-atl weight and fragment showing hole drilled through the center, presumably for the projectile shaft. *(Complete specimen is from Dade County; broken specimen is from Jenkins County. From a private collection)* **Photo No. 22**

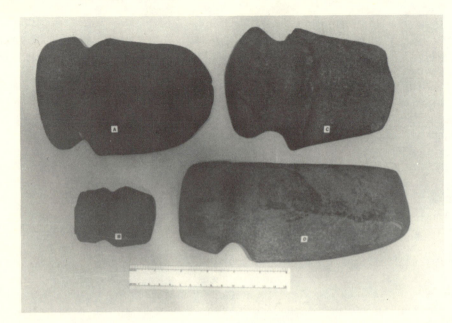

Grooved axes from various sites in Georgia. All have been smoothed by grinding. *(A & B, Clarke County; C, White County; D, Union County. From a private collection)* **Photo No. 23**

Perforated steatite (soapstone) slabs, generally thought to have been used in cooking. *(Northeast Georgia; from a private collection)* **Photo No. 24**

Savannah River projectile points are found widely in Georgia. *(Union County; from a private collection)* Photo No. 25

Savannah River stone knives. *(Union County; from a private collection)* Photo no. 26

In later excavations at the Stallings Island mound, Bullen and Greene (1970) duplicated many of Claflin's findings. Charcoal and charred plant remains from a pit about eighteen inches below the lowest potsherd in the pit yielded a date of 2,500 B.C. This and another similar date from the lowest zone of the site suggests a beginning date of 2,500-2,750 B.C. for the Stallings Island site (*op. cit.*:12).

Perhaps the most significant discovery in the excavations at Stallings Island had to do with the pottery made by the early inhabitants of the site. While some of the pottery in the topmost levels of the site belonged to later peoples who visited this location, the earliest pottery was quite different. Now known to represent the earliest pottery in the Southeast, it occurs along the Georgia coast and up the Savannah River, and on adjacent portions of the South Carolina and Florida coasts. The earliest examples of this pottery are undecorated, thick, and fiber-tempered. The tempering agent is variously identified as palmetto fiber, Spanish moss, pine needles, or other vegetable matter. Some or all were probably used, depending on what was readily available to the potter. The vessels were constructed by moulding them into shape rather than using the rope-coil method of construction. Somewhat later, vessels began to be decorated with simple punctate designs in the form of half-moons, circles, and slight curves. Hollow reeds, sticks, or bone tools may have been used in executing these designs (Bullen and Greene *op. cit.*:16). Another form of decoration introduced was the "stab-and drag" form of linear punctation. Bullen and Green (*ibid.*) say that this method of decoration "was applied by pushing the tool in at an angle . . . it was 'dragged' back and then pushed in again almost directly behind the previous mark." Such designs were applied to the soft clay prior to firing.

The significance of this pottery is far-reaching. Prior to this time, vessels were made of soapstone, a material which is locally common throughout the Piedmont and in the mountains. Soapstone quarries have been located by archaeologists in numerous counties, some of the most widely known being in the Atlanta area, particularly Soapstone Ridge. Soapstone vessels were chipped out in the round from the boulder or bedrock, detached at the base, and then hollowed out. Soapstone bowl fragments are relatively common finds on Late Archaic sites, but complete vessels are rare. The early pottery vessels at Stallings Island and on the coast copy the earlier soapstone vessels in form. Unlike the vessels of stone, pottery vessels were lighter and could be made from materials locally available. Soapstone vessels and perforated slabs, on the other hand, appear to have been traded by aboriginal inhabitants in the Piedmont to peoples living in the Coastal Plain, where steatite (soapstone) does not occur naturally.

A site on the Georgia coast which has yielded artifacts very similar to those found at Stallings Island is the Bilbo site near Savannah. This site was excavated as part of a WPA project and was supervised by Joseph R. Caldwell. The site was located just east of the city of Savannah in the middle of what was originally a brackish tidal swamp about one-half mile wide (Waring in Williams 1965:152). A small creek once flowed through this swamp and the Bilbo site was situated near this stream. At the time of excavation, the lowlands here had long since been drained and were in pasture, although just underneath the surface, muck was still to be found. A seventy-five-foot trench was excavated and two side trenches were then cut into the body of the deposit.

Plain fiber-tempered pottery sherd from the Georgia coastal region. *(Liberty County; from a private collection)* Photo No. 27

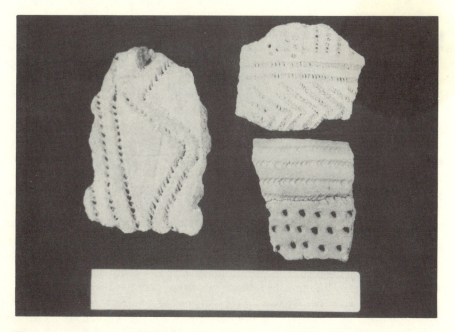

Fiber-tempered pottery exhibiting punctate or "stab and drag" decorations. *(Jenkins County; from a private collection)* Photo No. 28

Excellent stratigraphy existed, for the site consisted of a low mound which had grown from the swamp by a process of midden accumulation. At the time of excavation, this mound was about three feet higher than the surrounding lowland, although the midden accumulation was more than six feet thick in the center of the deposit.

Four distinct depositional zones were defined by the excavations. Zone No. 1 was the deepest level at the site and consisted of a uniform layer of oyster shell underlaying the entire mound and varying in thickness from ten to twenty inches (*op. cit.*: 155). The only artifacts recovered from this level were a bone awl, a perforated steatite slab, a perforated conch shell, and a ball of baked clay (*ibid.*).

Zone No. 2 was a black, midden-stained river deposit varying from six to twelve inches in depth and was immediately overlaying Zone No. 1. Found here was a small amount of fiber-tempered pottery, most of it undecorated, and numerous artifacts of chipped flint and bone. Some sixteen projectile points, square-stemmed with triangular blades, were among the artifacts recovered from this level. Made of flint, jasper, or slate, they are the same type as many from the Stallings Island site (see Warring *op. cit.*:173). Several clay-lined pits were also found in this level.

Midden Zone No. 3 was separated from Zone No. 2 by a foot or more of river gravel. Zone No. 3 consisted of dense, hard-packed layers of mussel and oyster shell, sand, and ash. These layers contained animal bone, artifacts of chipped flint and bone, and numerous sherds of both plain and decorated fiber-tempered pottery. This level was overlaid by Zone No. 4, which was arbitrarily declared to be the top fifteen inches of the deposit. This seemed to be the lower limits of the plow zone and contained nails, chinaware fragments, and sand-tempered potsherds (*ibid.*). Several pits and hearths were found in Zones 3 and 4. The hearths consisted of shallow depressions filled with burnt sand, charcoal, and ash cemented into a mass by the leachings from burned shell. Occasionally, fire-blackened stones were encountered, and one group of large pebbles found in a pit exhibited evidence of hammering. In all the excavations, no evidence of structures was found. A few scattered postholes were defined, but they formed no pattern (p. 156).

Waring (*op. cit.*:156-7) makes some interesting comments about the animal and human bone found in this excavation. The animal bone had been pounded into small splinters and bone and antler fragments frequently exhibited cut ends and knife scratches. Whole long bones were absent entirely and Waring notes: "One had a feeling that these remains were deposited by a group who depended on hunting and fishing to a marked degree and who systematically utilized every scrap of extractable food material" (*ibid.*). The lower levels of the site contained large quantities of hickory nut shells, indicating that gathering played a role in the economy. At least fifteen fragments of human bone were recovered, none in a burial situation. All human bones were cracked, some had been burned, and some bore cuts (p. 245).

One of the most valuable results of the excavation of the Bilbo site was the definition of the pottery sequence for this part of the coast. The fiber-tempered sherds indicated that the complete vessel was large, slab-sided, with a straight or slightly incurving rim. The bottoms were flat and all evidence indicates that the vessels were made by moulding, and not by the rope-coil method. The types defined by Waring include St. Simons Punctated, St. Simons Incised, and St. Simons Plain (see Waring *op. cit.*:160). He justifies a nomenclature different from that of Stallings

Island because the ceramics at the Bilbo site are thicker than Stallings Island vessels; the punctated decorations of the Stallings Island vessels are smaller, neater, and more varied than those at the Bilbo site; some Stallings Island vessels bear a crude form of simple stamped decoration; and vessel shapes were different at the two sites. The stratigraphic evidence at the Bilbo site suggests that undecorated fiber-tempered pottery preceded the decorated wares on the Georgia coast.

Other artifact types recovered at this location include thirteen antler projectile points, five awls made from deer ulnae, twenty-five awls made from splinters of deer long bone, some eighty-five bone pins, some of which are engraved, a bone fishhook, and some miscellaneous bone objects. Stone artifacts include quartzite pebbles, pitted stones, fragments of steatite bowls, and perforated steatite slabs.

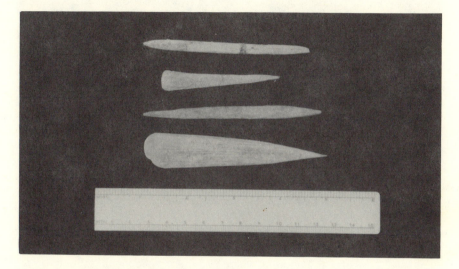

Bone pins or awls, commonly found in Archaic shell middens. *(Jenkins County; from a private collection)* Photo No. 29

The ancient inhabitants of the Bilbo site could exploit both the fresh-water swamp and the salt-water marsh for edible species. The quantities of animal bone, noticeably deer, the mollusc shells, turtle and sturgeon bones, and the hickory nut remains all attest to their hunting, gathering, and fishing activities in the vicinity.

The material culture represented in the pre-ceramic levels at the Stallings Island site is found widely in Georgia and the Southeast. In the Piedmont of North Carolina, Coe (*op. cit.*:44-5, 54-5) found abundant Savannah River points, as well as large quarry blades, at the Doerschuk site. He estimates that this level dates from about 2,000 B.C. In the mountains of North Carolina, Savannah River points are present on practically every site and form the dominant component at some sites, particularly those at higher elevations (see White 1972). This same projectile point type is found widely in South Carolina and Alabama, associated with the Late Archaic occupation in each case.

There is one other type of archaeological site which must be discussed, and it is included here not because it necessarily belongs to the Archaic period, but, because

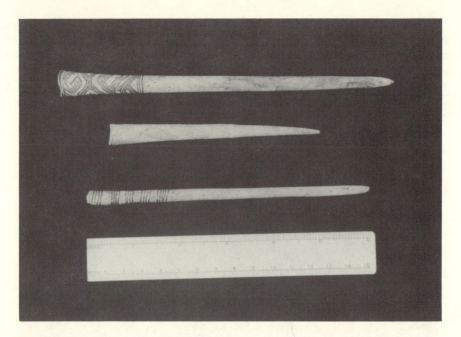

Engraved bone pins from a late Archaic shell midden. *(Jenkins County; from a private collection)* **Photo No. 30**

Archaic peoples utilized soapstone perhaps more than later peoples, the probability of association with this time period is rather strong. I am speaking of the rocks, boulders, and stone outcrops with petroglyphs. These objects are found widely in the Southeast, and it is easier to say what they are not than to say what they are. Almost always executed on soapstone boulders, the variety of symbols, lines, dots, and tracks are not some kind of map indicating where treasure is to be found ("if only we could read it"), nor are they any kind of written message. Several of these petroglypic rocks figure in Indian legends, such as those at Trackrock Gap near Young Harris. Archaeologists have found it very difficult to assign these artifacts to any cultural period because there is nothing associated with them which would give a clue as to the time period to which they belong. Some of the carvings, such as circles with a dot in the middle, turkey tracks (?), and holes drilled into the rock to a depth of an inch or so, are common petroglyphs throughout the area. They probably represent ritual symbols shared by peoples living in this region, but they are not treasure maps or messages for future generations to decipher.

Late Archaic: A Summary

By the profusion of artifacts associated with the late Archaic in Georgia, it is evident that peoples throughout the state were efficiently exploiting food resources in every region. Particularly plentiful are late Archaic sites along the coast. It should be pointed out that earlier Archaic sites are not much in evidence along the coast because of a rise in sea level during the last few thousand years. Thus, Paleo-Indian and early to middle Archaic sites in this area are mostly inundated. But with late Archaic times, sea level was more or less at modern limits and archaeological sites are found all along the coast.

The hunting, gathering, and fishing activities of coastal peoples at this time can only be inferred from floral, faunal, and artifactual remains. Since stone suitable for manufacturing projectile points is not locally available, stone projectile points are not common along the coast. However, socketed antler points have been found at numerous coastal sites, including shell middens. A few stone scrapers and knives, along with some atl-atl weights, have been found in coastal sites, the latter furnishing evidence of the use of the throwing-stick in the area.

There is not direct evidence of the use of nets or traps in fishing, but concentrations of extremely small fish vertebrae are encountered in the excavation of coastal shell middens. Thus, at least one researcher has argued for the use of some form of net or woven basketry trap (see DePratter 1979:16). A shell tool which is commonly found in coastal shell middens is a whelk shell which is either sharpened or battered on the distal end, and containing what is apparently a hafting hole in the outer whorl. We can only speculate as to the use of these artifacts, but the holes and distal ends of many exhibit considerable wear. It has been suggested that they were used as digging tools or as wood-working implements, especially for use with fire in manufacturing dugout canoes. In the latter case, controlled burning of portions of the log was followed by chipping away the charred area, eventually resulting in a dugout canoe.

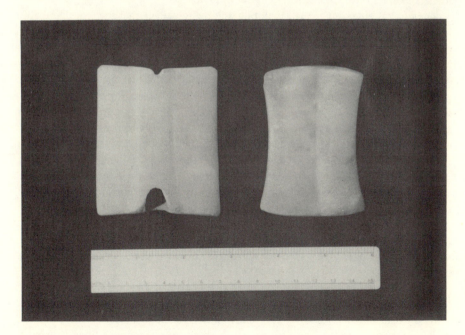

Atl-atl weights, also called "bannerstones." *(Left to right: Emanuel County, Talbot County; from a private collection)* **Photo No. 31**

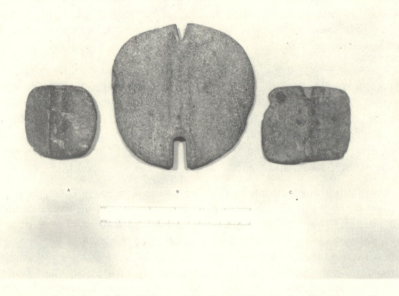

Various types of atl-atl weights. *(Left to right: Towns County, Lincoln County, Union County; from a private collection)* **Photo No. 32**

Finally, one researcher has suggested that these shell tools may have been used as hammers in cracking open clams (DePratter *op. cit.*)

The coastal environment is a rich one and many believe that the varied and abundant food sources found there would have enabled late Archaic hunters and gatherers to remain on or near the coast year-round. DePratter (1979:20-27) discusses some of the subsistence data obtained from excavations of coastal sites, coupled with his own extensive knowledge of the coast. He delineates three natural zones in the coastal region: the marsh/lagoon, the maritime forest, and the beach/open sea. Each zone has its own distinctive life forms, many of which were and are economically important. Excavation of archaeological sites has enabled archaeologists to identify many of the species exploited by prehistoric coastal dwellers. Thus, we know that late Archaic populations exploited the following molluscs, all found in the marsh/lagoon: oysters (*Crassostrea virginica* Gmelin), clams (*Mercenaria mercenaria* L.), conch or whelk species (*Busycon contrarium, B. canaliculatum* L., *B. carica* Gmelin), ribbed mussels (*Modiolus demissus*), and marsh periwinkle (*Littorina irrorata*). Little or no specialized equipment would have been required in harvesting these food sources (see DePratter *op. cit.*). The only crustacean remains found in archaeological sites along the coast are claws of the blue crab, which is abundant in the marshes from spring through early fall.

Fish remains are commonly found in the coastal shell middens, but few have been identified as to species. The most extensive work in this respect has been conducted on fish remains from two sites on St. Simons Island (Marrinan 1975). Of thirty species represented in the fish remains from these two sites, only three (freshwater catfish, bowfin, and bass) are freshwater species. All the others are found in tidal creeks and rivers, and menhaden, marine catfish, drum, and mullet were determined to have been the most important species for the peoples living in this region during late Archaic times (*op. cit.*).

The open sea/beach zone is represented only by sea turtle remains, which are rare in the archaeological record (DePratter *op. cit.*), but the maritime forest zone contained several species of animals which were important to late Archaic peoples. Among these are the white-tailed deer (*Odocoileus virginianus*), raccoon (*Procyon lotor*), opossum (*Didelphis virginiana*), marsh rabbit (*Sylvilagus palustris*), cottontail rabbit (*S. floridanus*). and wild turkey (*Meleagris gallopavo*). Remains of all these species have been found in shell middens of the late Archaic, but not in large numbers. Because of this situation, Caldwell (1958:14) argues that during some seasons, probably fall and winter, the people "would have retired into the back country as in historic times, probably preferring the valleys of the major streams to the more barren lands between them." In a survey conducted in the interior of McIntosh and Long Counties, a total of 171 sites were found. Of these, 37 sites contained late Archaic fiber-tempered ceramics (Zurel, et al. 1975). This survey demonstrated the presence of late Archaic peoples in the interior sections of the coastal region, but the information as presented in this report gives little insight into what economic activities may be represented at these sites.

While most sites along the coast are in the form of shell middens or artifact scatters, a few sites are marked by large rings of shell. These shell rings have variously been interpreted as representing some ceremonial activity or as being the build-up of refuse around a circular dwelling. At any rate, the interior of these rings is generally devoid of artifacts. The exact purpose of shell rings remains unknown.

Farther inland on the Coastal Plain, a University of Georgia survey in 1976 yielded some surprises. Before this survey, it was assumed that the "pine barrens" were of little or no use to native inhabitants of the area. However, some eighty-nine archaeological sites were located by this survey in portions of Grady and Mitchell Counties. Artifacts revealed that the most intense occupation of the area occurred during the late Archaic (Fish and Mitchell 1976:11). Of the artifacts recovered, a large proportion were projectile points. Nearly all were late Archaic types, with the Savannah River point being present. Many of these projectile points were made from non-local materials, indicating that these sites were probably hunting camps belonging to groups of people who lived outside of the immediate area (*op. cit.*:21). Further evidence of hunting activities is the presence of choppers, scrapers and large bifaces.

Most of the sites discovered in this survey were located in the boundary area between the Dougherty Plain and the Solution Escarpment. This area would have made resources in both microenvironments available to prehistoric peoples. Only one site was found on the Dougherty Plain itself, and it was near a large natural sink, which contained especially rich resources in its vicinity (*op. cit.*) The Escarpment/Plain boundary is marked in vegetation. While sites representing all other time periods are known in this area, late Archaic sites are the most numerous.

To the north, the Sand Hills region of the innermost Coastal Plain has formed another little-known area from an archaeological standpoint. A 1980 survey of cultural resources on the Fort Gordon Military Reservation has shed considerable light on the prehistory of the region and has opened up new avenues for interpreting aboriginal

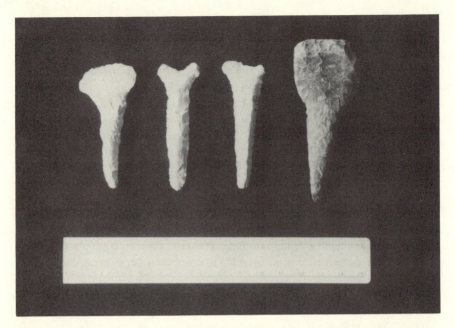

Drills found on Archaic sites in Georgia. *(Left to right: Calhoun County, Baldwin County, Calhoun County, and Terrell County; from a private collection)* **Photo No. 33**

land use, particularly during the late Archaic. A fact which surprised the survey team was the presence of Stalling Island materials in a non-riverine setting, demonstraing use of the hinterland by people at this time. Stallings Island projectile points, fiber-tempered ceramics, perforated steatite slabs, scrapers, manos, metates, hammerstones, and mortar basins were all found by this survey. The plant-food processing equipment suggests that the upland region subsistence pattern was quite different from that represented along the river (Campbell et al. 1980). While the riverine sites are clearly oriented toward collecting shellfish and hunting deer, the upland sites were oriented toward the intensive gathering of plant foods, primarily nuts (*op. cit.*).

In the Piedmont and mountains, late Archaic sites are ubiquitous, being found in the riverbottoms, along ridges, and in mountain gaps. This situation certainly demonstrates an intensive use of resources in varying life zones or microenvironments and indicates a substantial human population at this time. Evidence found on these sites is associated with hunting and butchering as well as plant collecting and processing.

The late Archaic saw the appearance of two traits, both of which were to prove of tremendous importance to peoples in succeeding time periods. These two traits are pottery vessels and horticulture. Presumably, the increasing reliance on plant foods during the middle Archaic led Indians in some areas to begin intensively exploiting the seeds of certain plants, eventually leading to the cultivation and/or domestication of the plant. The increasing sedentism, originating in the scheduling of subsistence activities so that population movement was minimized, is thought to have been a vital step in plant cultivation, for the people lived in the same place for several months each year. Thus, sunflower and amaranth seeds appear in the archaeological record in late Archaic sites in Tennessee, Kentucky, and other states. Both were native North American cultigens, but the squash, also appearing in the late Archaic, is native to Central America and probably reached the Southeast by trade. The development of horticulture and the spread of pottery-making usher in the next period in Georgia prehistory—the Woodland Period.

REFERENCES: CHAPTER IV

Anderson, David G., Sammy T. Lee, and A. Robert Parler, *Cal Smoak: Archaeological Investiga-*
1979   *tions Along the Edisto River in the Coastal Plain of South Carolina,* Archaeological Society of South Carolina, Occasional Papers 1.

————————————, and Joseph Schuldenrein, "Archaeological Investigations at Ruck-
1981   er's Bottom, Elbert County, Georgia," Paper presented at the 38th Southeastern Archaeological Conference, Asheville, North Carolina.

————————————————————, "Early Archaic Settlement on the
1983   Southeastern Atlantic Slope: A View from the Rucker's Bottom Site, Elbert County, Georgia," *North American Archaeologist,* Vol. 4, No. 3, pp. 177-210.

Brockington, P.B., "A Preliminary Investigation of an Early Knapping Site in Southeastern Geor-
1971   gia," *The Notebook, Institute of Archaeology and Anthropology, University of South Carolina,* Vol. III, pp. 34-46.

Broyles, Bettye J., *Second Preliminary Report: The St. Albans Site, Kanawha County, West Vir-*
1971   *ginia,* Report of Archaeological Investigations No. 3, West Virginia Geological and Economic Survey, Morgantown.

Bullen, Ripley P., and H. Bruce Greene, "Stratigraphic Tests at Stallings Island, Georgia," *Florida*
1970   *Anthropologist,* No. 23, pp. 8-28.

Caldwell, Joseph R., "The Old Quartz Industry of Piedmont Georgia and South Carolina," *South-*
1954   *ern Indian Studies,* No. 6, pp. 27-39.

————————————, *Trend and Tradition in the Prehistory of the Eastern United States,*
1958   American Anthropological Association, Memoir 88.

————————————, "Appraisal of the Archaeological Resources of Hartwell Reservoir,
1974   South Carolina and Georgia," *Institute of Archaeology and Anthropology, University of South Carolina, The Notebook,* Vol. 6, No. 2, pp. 35-44.

Cambron, J.W., and S.A. Waters, "Flint Creek Rock Shelter (Part I)," *Tennessee Archaeologist,*
1959   Vol. 15, pp. 73-87.

Campbell, Janice L., Carol S. Weed, and Prentice M. Thomas, Jr., *Archaeological Investigations at*
1981   *the Fort Gordon Military Reservation, Georgia,* Report of Investigations No. 33, New World Research, Inc.

Chapman, Jefferson, "The Archaic Period in the Lower Little Tennessee River Valley: The Radio-
1976   carbon Dates," *Tennessee Anthropologist,* Vol. 1, No. 1, pp. 1-12.

Claflin, W.H., Jr., "The Stallings Island Mound, Columbia County, Georgia," *Papers of the Peabody*
1931   *Museum of American Archaeology and Ethnology, No. 14.*

Clausen, Carl J., A.D. Cohen, Cesare Emiliani, J.A. Holman, and J.J. Stipp, "Little Salt Spring,
1979   Florida: A Unique Underwater Site," *Science,* No. 203, pp. 609-614.

Coe, Joffre L., *The Formative Cultures of the Carolina Piedmont,* Transactions of the American
1964   Philosophical Society, New Series, Vol. 54, Philadelphia.

DePratter, Chester B., "The Archaic in Georgia," *Early Georgia,* Vol. 3, No. 1, pp. 1-16.
1975

————————————, "Shellmound Archaic on the Georgia Coast," *South Carolina*
1979   *Antiquities,* Vol. 2, No. 2, Archaeological Society of South Carolina, Columbia.

Dickens, Roy S., Jr., "The Stone Mountain Salvage Project, DeKalb and Gwinnett Counties,
1964   Georgia," *Journal of Alabama Archaeology*, Vol. 10, pp. 43-49.

Fish, Paul R., and William W. Mitchell, *Late Archaic Settlement in the Big Slough Watershed:*
1976   *Results of an Archaeological Survey for the U.S.D.A. Soil Conservation Service in Grady
        and Mitchell Counties, Georgia*, University of Georgia Laboratory of Archaeology Series,
        Report No. 13, Athens.

Fish, Suzanne K., Paul R. Fish, and Richard W. Jefferies, *An Examination of Interfluvial Settle-*
1978   *ment in the Georgia Southern Piedmont: The Georgia Power Company Plant Scherer
        Archaeological Survey*, University of Georgia Laboratory of Archaeology Series, Report
        No. 15, Athens.

Fowler, M.L., "Modoc Rock Shelter: An Early Archaic Site in Southern Illinois," *American
1959   Antiquity*, Vol. 24, pp. 257-270.

Goodyear, Albert C., James L. Michie, and Barbara A. Purdy, "The Edgefield Scraper: A Distri-
1980   butional Study of an Early Archaic Stone Tool from the Southeastern U.S.," Paper
        presented at the 37th Annual Southeastern Archaeological Conference, New Orleans.

Huscher, Harold A., "The Standing Boy Flint Industry: An Early Archaic Manifestation of the
1964   Chattahoochee River in Alabama and Georgia," *Southern Indian Studies*, Vol. XVI, pp.
        3-20.

Hutto, Brooks, *Archaeological Survey of the Elbert County, Georgia, Portion of the Proposed
1970   Trotters Shoals Reservoir, Savannah River*, University of Georgia Laboratory of Arch-
        aeology Series, No. 7.

Kellar, James H., and Edward V. McMichaels, *Archaeological Salvage in the Oliver Basin*, Uni-
1960   versity of Georgia Laboratory of Archaeology Series, Report No. 2.

Jones, Charles C., *Antiquities of the Southern Indians, Particularly of the Georgia Tribes*, D. Apple-
1873   ton and Co., New York.

Lewis, Thomas M.N., and Madeline Kneberg Lewis, *Eva, an Archaic Site*, University of Tennessee
1961   Study in Anthropology, University of Tennessee Press, Knoxville.

Marrinan, Rochelle, "Ceramics, Molluscs, and Sedentism: The Late Archaic Period on the Georgia
1975   Coast,' Unpublished Ph.D. Dissertation, University of Florida, Gainesville.

Michie, James L., "The Taylor Point," *The Chesopiean*, Vol. 4, No. 5 and 6, pp. 123-124.
1966

_____, "The Edgefield Scraper: A Tool of Inferred Antiquity and Use,"
1972   *Southeastern Archaeological Conference, Bulletin 15*, ed. by Bettye J. Broyles, Morgan-
        town, West Virginia, pp. 84-90.

Milanich, Jerald T., and Charles H. Fairbanks, *Florida Archaeology*, Academic Press, Inc., New
1980   York.

Neill, Wilfred T., "Westo Bluff, A Site of the Old Quartz Culture," *Florida Anthropologist*, Vol.
1966   19, pp. 1-10.

Schneider, Kent A., "Microsample Extraction: Innovative Instrumentation for Archeological Data
1972   Recovery," Unpublished Ph.D. Dissertation, University of Georgia, Athens.

Struever, Stuart, "Flotation Techniques for the Recovery of Small-scale Archaeological Remains,"
1968   *American Antiquity*, Vol. 33, pp. 353-62.

Taylor, Richard L., and Marion F. Smith, *The Report of the Intensive Survey of the Richard B.
1978   Russell Dam and Lake, Savannah River, Georgia and South Carolina*, Research Manu-
        script Series 142, Institute of Archaeology and Anthropology, University of South Caro-
        lina, Columbia.

Tippitt, V. Ann, and William H. Marquardt, *The Gregg Shoals and Clyde Gulley Sites: Archaeolo-
1984   gical and Geological Investigations at Two Piedmont Sites on the Savannah River*, Russell
        Papers, Archaeological Services, National Park Service, Atlanta.

Tuck, James A., "Early Archaic Horizons in Eastern North America," *Archaeology of Eastern
1974   North America*, Vol. 2, No. 1, pp. 73-80.

Walthall, John A., *Prehistoric Indians of the Southeast: Archaeology of Alabama and the Middle
1980   South*, University of Alabama Press, University, Alabama.

Warner, Richard A., "The Griffin Site: A Stratified Archaic Site from Northwest Georgia," Paper
1974   presented at the Georgia Academy of Science Meeting.

Watts, W.A., "Postglacial and Interglacial Vegetation History of Southern Georgia and Central
1971   Florida," *Ecology,* Vol. 52, pp. 676-690.

_____, "Late Quaternary Vegetation History at White Pond on the Inner
1980   Coastal Plain of South Carolina," *Quaternary Research,* Vol. 13, No. 2, pp. 187-199.

White, Max E., "Excavations at the Evans Gap Site, Jackson County, North Carolina," Paper
1972   presented at the Southeastern Archaeological Conference, Macon, Georgia.

_____, "An Early Site in Banks County, Georgia," Paper presented at
1982   the meeting of the Society for Georgia Archaeology, Athens, Georgia.

Willey, Gordon R., *An Introduction to American Archaeology, Vol. I: North and Middle America,*
1966   Prentice-Hall, Inc., Englewood Cliffs, New Jersey.

Williams, Stephen, ed., *The Waring Papers: The Southern Cult and Other Archaeological Essays,*
1965   by Antonio J. Waring, Jr., University of Georgia Press, Athens.

Zurel, Richard, T. Gresham, and David Hally, *An Archaeological Survey of Channel, Dike, and*
1975   *Streambank Protection Structures, Big Mortar-Snuffbox Swamp Watershed, Long and*
        McIntosh Counties, Georgia, University of Georgia Laboratory of Archaeology, Research
        Manuscript No. 116, Athens.

Chapter V

THE WOODLAND PERIOD
1000 B.C.–A.D. 1000

*I*n Georgia and throughout the Southeast, the basic lifeway established during the Archaic continued with an exception—freshwater shellfish virtually disappeared from the diet and thus from the archaeological record along the larger inland streams. The fact that shellfish ceased to be a major food source for peoples living along the inland rivers was directly caused by the higher water level in the rivers, which rendered the mussels inaccessible. The higher water level had in turn been caused by the more modern, wetter climate following the Altithermal. While this situation caused a reorientation of subsistence strategies for peoples who formerly exploited the freshwater shellfish, those groups living in the Coastal Plains, Piedmont, and mountains were evidently little affected. Even those for whom shellfish had been an important dietary element apparently were able to survive quite well without them.

Plant cultivation, which appeared in the late Archaic, continued to be of little economic importance in the Woodland Period, despite the addition of maize to those plants being cultivated. From all that archaeologists can determine, plant cultivation provided only an additional source of food to late Archaic and Woodland peoples. They could, and many perhaps did, get along without it. But if little change in subsistence is seen, there is considerable change in other respects, notably in technology and later, in ceremonialism as Georgia peoples began to be influenced by a vigorous cultural development in the Midwest.

Perhaps the most important identifier of early Woodland sites is the pottery. The fiber-tempered, molded vessels of the late Archaic gave way to vessels which were sand-tempered, constructed by the rope-coil method, and decorated in a variety of ways. This change in ceramic style, initially marked by the addition of sand or grit tempering to the fiber temper, began on the Georgia coast about 1100 B.C. and resulted in the eventual replacement of vegetable fibers by sand or grit. This event gives rise to the pottery associated with the early Woodland Refuge phase along the coast and inland in the Coastal Plain. The Refuge site, located just across the Savannah River in Jasper County, South Carolina, was excavated in 1947. Recently, another site nearby was excavated by a team from the University of South Carolina-Beaufort campus (Lepionka 1983). These and other excavations enabled archaeologists to describe

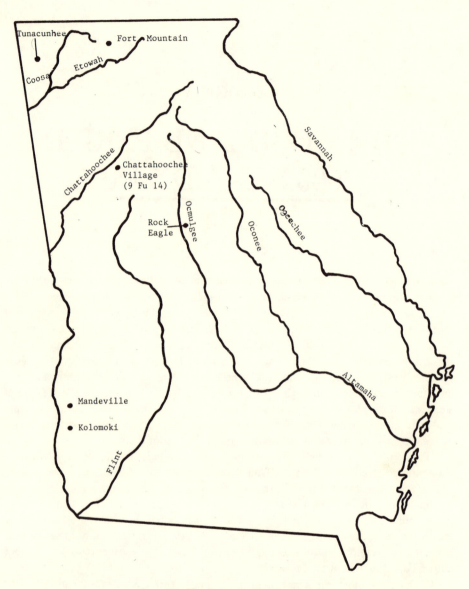

Some Woodland sites in Georgia. Map 5

the pottery types associated with the Refuge Phase, but no burials or house plans were found and little is known about the subsistence. There are inferences, however, which will be discussed below.

The earliest Refuge ceramics are described as being either plain or decorated with a punctate or incised method. A dentate stamped design is present on some sherds, and somewhat later crude simple stamping, consisting of impressed lines, was introduced. Vessels were broad-based with rounded bottoms (Lepionka *op. cit.*). Detailed descriptions of the Refuge pottery types can be found in Lepionka (*op. cit.*) and DePratter (1979).

Regrettably, our knowledge of the life of these early Woodland inhabitants of the coastal region is limited. This may be due in part to the inundation of coastal sites, for studies by the University of Florida on St. Simons Island indicate a rise in ocean level of some three feet since about 1000 B.C. The original site, excavated by Waring (see Williams 1968), consisted of an eroding midden of freshwater mussel shells. This indicates the use of freshwater shellfish in the diet, but neither this nor other articles on the Refuge phase mention any other faunal remains. That Refuge phase sites are found inland on the Coastal Plain is suggestive of seasonal exploitation of resources in this area. Sites are small and contain no midden (see DePratter 1976), indicating short-term occupation.

While the making of fiber-tempered ceramics apparently spread from the Savannah River and coastal areas through the Coastal Plain, such ceramics are extremely rare or non-existent in the Piedmont and northward. Only a few sites near the Savannah River in the central and lower Piedmont bear fiber-tempered sherds. In northern Georgia, the earliest ceramics were grit or sand-tempered and bore decorations applied by pressing a stick or paddle wrapped in fabric to the vessel surface. This technique yielded what is called the Dunlap fabric-marked pottery, a type found on some sites in the Piedmont, mountains, and into the Coastal Plain. This technique of pottery decoration appears to have been derived from the north, and indeed Caldwell (1958:23-25) believed that it very possibly represents evidence of a migration of peoples from the Midwest.

Potsherd bearing Dunlap fabric-marked decorations. The drilled hole was probably for a thong for hanging or carrying the vessel. *(Union County; from a private collection)* **Photo No. 34**

Dunlap fabric-marked ceramics are associated with what Caldwell called the Kellog focus. Associated traits include a medium-sized triangular projectile point with a slightly concave base. Their small size (see photo 46 on page 90) led Caldwell to suggest their use as arrowheads rather than as dart-points for the atl-atl. He speculates that the two-holed bar gorgets also found at this time may have been used as wrist-guards, if indeed the bow and arrow were being used. Other types of artifacts appearing at this time include tubular pipes, grinding slabs, and the enigmatic boatstones. One of the outstanding traits of the Kellog focus is the use of cylindrical or bell-shaped pits two to five feet in diameter in which carbonized remains of acorns, hickory nuts, and walnuts were found (Caldwell nd.). This is indicative of the dependence on forest resources, and Caldwell speculates that this cultural expression represented an adaptation to life in the mixed deciduous forest of the Piedmont and mountains and northward. Indeed, sites containing Dunlap fabric-marked pottery are very rare below the Fall Line, but they have been found as far south as the Mandeville site in Clay County (Kellar et al. 1962:341).

A few house structures and burials associated with the Kellog focus have been excavated. At a site in Bartow County, Wauchope uncovered a round house structure some twenty-four feet in diameter (Wauchope 1966; Garrow 1975). Burials were normally flexed and placed in circular or semi-circular graves. Based on radiocarbon dates from Kellog focus sites, Garrow (*op. cit.*:20) assigns tentative dates for the Kellog focus of 1000-300 B.C. This is in keeping with dates from the Mahan site in Gordon County, where material associated with Dunlap fabric-marked ceramics yielded dates of 540 B.C. and 636 B.C. A site in Cherokee County yielded dates of 565 B.C. and 470 B.C. (Bowen 1982:36).

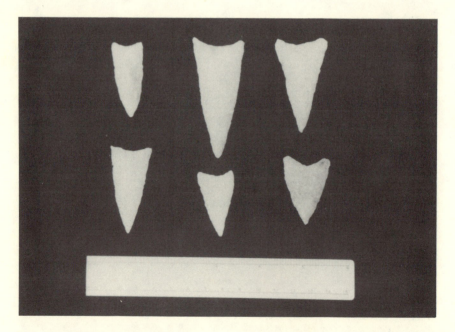

Typical Woodland projectile points. These specimens are made of quartz. *(Lumpkin County; from a private collection)* Photo No. 35

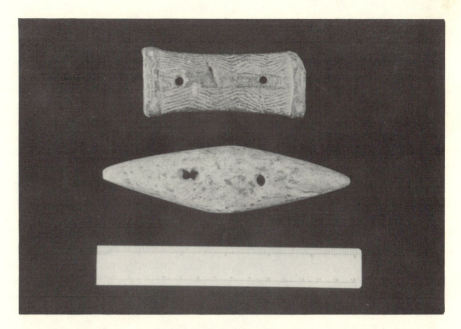

Two-holed bar gorgets, associated with the early Woodland occupation of parts of Georgia. *(Top specimen is from Bartow County; other is from DeKalb County; from a private collection)* Photo No. 36

A tubular pipe made of soapstone. *(Union County; from a private collection)* Photo No. 37

Most of the sites of the Kellog focus are situated in riverbottoms. Substantial house structures, as well as storage and cooking pits are all indicative of a more sedentary population. Few sites associated with this period are known from upland or highland situations, but occasionally Dunlap fabric-marked pottery is found on such sites. What is evidently reflected by this patterning is a highly sedentary population with an economy based on intensive exploitation of floral and faunal resources of the oak-hickory forest. Hoes made of slate and showing wear were found on a site from this time period in Cherokee County and may indicate plant cultivation (Bowen *op. cit.*).

It was during the last few centuries B.C. that a vigorous culture was developing in the Ohio Valley area, one which would profoundly influence peoples in Georgia and other areas of the eastern United States. The so-called Adena culture is the first expression of this cultural florescence. Found along the Ohio River from Indiana eastward, Adena sites are marked by burial mounds and earthwork enclosures. The burial mounds are conical and vary in size, and the earthworks are generally interpreted as ceremonial rather than defensive works. Elaborate mortuary customs are evident in Adena burials, for important individuals were buried in log tombs, over which an earth mound was built. Red ochre was sometimes rubbed onto the bones, indicating that either the flesh was stripped from the skeleton or it was allowed to decay and the ochre was applied later (Willey 1966:269).

The Adena culture gave rise to the Hopewell culture, the highest cultural development in North America up to that time. The basic pattern of small villages, hunting, gathering, fishing, and limited plant cultivation continued, but changes are seen in the ceremonial life of the people. Earthworks dating from the Hopewell era are larger and more complex than those of the Adena culture. The earthworks sometimes enclose hundreds of acres, are often geometric, and most seem not to have been defensive in nature. Burial mounds are often associated with them. There are some earthworks, however, that give the appearance of having served as fortifications. In these instances, walls of earth or stones encircled hilltops, often following the natural terrain in a manner which suggests their use as defensive embankments (Willey *op. cit.*).

Hopewell burials were even more elaborate than those of the Adena. Log tombs were still used for important individuals, and earth mounds, some very large, were erected over these tombs. Exotic goods, evidence of widespread trade with peoples in other areas, were placed with these important burials. Objects made of mica (Southern Appalachians), copper (Great Lakes), obsidian (Yellowstone National Park), and conch shell (Gulf Coast) are among those found in Hopewell burials. Effigy pipes, stone ear spools, carved human and animal bones, pottery vessels, and clay human figurines are also found (see photos 39, 42 and 45 on pages 80, 85, and 90 respectively). The figurines present a view of how the Hopewell peoples looked and dressed. The pottery is typically decorated in a manner called rocker-stamping, and often includes zoned patterns. The Hopewell culture in the Ohio Valley reached its zenith in the period 100 B.C.-A.D. 200, and it is in this general time that Hopewellian influences appear in Georgia.

A site which shows strong Hopewell affinities is the Tunacunnhee site in Dade County, extreme northwest Georgia. The site is situated in the valley of Lookout Creek at the base of the Appalachian Plateau province. The four prehistoric mounds are located on a slightly elevated area in the floodplain, while the habitation area is situated between the mounds and Lookout Creek. Excavations were carried out by archaeologists from the University of Georgia in 1973. The large mound, Mound A, was found to be constructed almost entirely of limestone rocks and it measured thirty-seven feet north-south by forty feet east-west. The mound was four feet high at the time of excavation. The tumulus had been constructed over a large pit that had been excavated into the original ground surface. This pit contained burned bone fragments and a portion of a copper earspool, and was partially surrounded by a ring of red clay varying from one to four feet in width and about one foot thick (Jeffries 1976).

A view of the University of Georgia excavations at the Tunacunnhee site, Dade County. *(Courtesy Department of Anthropology, University of Georgia)* **Photo No. 38**

Mound C was a circular earth mound capped with a mantle of limestone rocks. A large rectangular pit at the base of the mound yielded a large mica disc. Nearby in the pit lay the remains of a fabric bag or folded cloth containing several copper artifacts. The copper salts had preserved portions of the fabric. The copper objects included a copper plate, two sets of earspools, and an awl or pin. The fabric remains yielded a radiocarbon date of A.D. 150. Also among the contents of this bag were beads made from small animal vertebrae, thirty-seven shark vertebrae, a drilled bear canine, and other small objects (Jefferies *op. cit.*). An adult male burial had been placed on top of the pit after it was filled. This burial contained a large mica cutout in the shape of a hook or claw, and seven bone pins.

In all, numerous artifacts were recovered from Tunacunnhee that are typical of Hopewell sites elsewhere. They include copper panpipes, which were generally found on

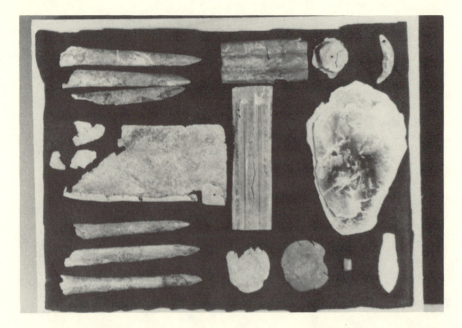

Objects from the Tunacunnhee site, including bone awls, beaten copper, pan pipes, mica, ear spools, and a perforated bear tooth. *(From a private collection)* **Photo No. 39**

the chest of a burial, copper earspools, a copper celt, platform and effigy pipes, bear canines, shark teeth, and two pottery vessels analogous to vessels found elsewhere in Hopewellian contexts.

Excavations in the village area at the site yielded the remains of postmoulds and some pits. One complete structure, a dwelling some ten feet in diameter with a rock-filled central pit, was excavated, and the author of the report speculates that this may have been a sweathouse (Jefferies *op. cit.*:19). Jefferies notes that the Tunacunnhee site is located near the Tennessee River in the vicinity of where several historic Indian trails converged. If these trails were used as long ago as the time of the Tunacunnhee site occupation, then its population would have been in a strategic location for trading. Furthermore, the site is situated near one of the few gaps where Lookout Mountain could be crossed. Certainly trading potential for exotic materials should be taken into account in interpreting the Tunacunnhee site in the overall Hopewell manifestation, for items from the Gulf Coast as well as the Southern Appalachians could have been procured here for transport to the Hopewell heartland in the Ohio Valley. Indeed, a prehistoric mica mine is known in Gordon County, several miles east of the Tuna-cunnhee site (Ferguson 1974), and native copper could have been obtained in the same general area.

Elsewhere in northern Georgia, this period is denoted by changes associated with what Caldwell called the Cartersville focus. Caldwell (1958:38) suggested a time range of A.D. 1-500 for this phase in north Georgia prehistory. He identified it on the basis of the appearance of simple-stamped and check-stamped ceramics along with the earlier fabric-marked and plain wares. Also, some complicated-stamped pottery (Swift

Creek), emanating from cultures in the Coastal Plain, appears in the archaeological record, but remains a minority type in this part of the state.

Early Woodland potsherds showing simple-stamped and check-stamped decoration. *(Banks County; from a private collection)* **Photo No. 40**

Potsherd bearing a typical Swift Creek motif. *(White County; from a private collection)* **Photo No. 41**

One of the most significant changes assigned to the Cartersville phase is an apparent shift in subsistence strategies which involved a decrease in the use of acorns and other nuts as major food resources. Caldwell found few storage pits on Cartersville sites in the course of his investigations in the Allatoona reservoir, but such pits were abundant on the earlier sites associated with the Kellog occupation. The cause of this economic shift has not been ascertained by archaeologists, but it does not seem to be assignable to an increasing dependence on cultivated plants, for there is no evidence that this pursuit had yet gained more than minimal importance. What is deemed as more likely is that the universal use of pottery cooking vessels meant that greater food value could be extracted from resources, unlike earlier preparation methods. If nuts are crushed, then boiled, there is greater nutritional value available, and fewer remains for the archaeological record. Thus, the absence of nut remains and the storage or cooking pits so common in the earlier Kellog phase should not necessarily be interpreted as a lesser use of this resource. It very possibly reflects merely a newer, more efficient use of the resource.

In his excavations in the Allatoona reservoir, Caldwell found the remains of several dwellings of the Cartersville occupation. He recorded structures that were circular and contained stone-lined pit hearths in the center. Hearths containing fire-cracked rocks were located outside of the dwellings (Caldwell 1958:46). As a result of industrial development, the remains of an entire Cartersville period village were discovered along the banks of the Chattahoochee River in Fulton County in 1969. Archaeologists eventually uncovered the remains of thirty house structures, distributed at random in the riverbottoms. The structures were round or oval-shaped, averaged fifteen feet in diameter, and were defined by dark postmoulds which sharply contrasted with the surrounding orange-red clay. Each dwelling exhibited a central hearth or cooking pit consisting of fire-cracked rocks, ash, and charcoal. A radiocarbon date from one such pit indicates occupation of the village about A.D. 214. Pottery further identified the village as belonging to the Cartersville period in north Georgia (Kelly 1973).

Faunal remains from Cartersville sites excavated by Kelly and Meier in 1969 and 1970, including the one just discussed, indicate exploitation of small mammals (raccoons, squirrels, rabbits, and opossums). Remains of hickory nuts and some seeds were also recovered, and Kelly (*op. cit.*:36) states that the two Cartersville period villages he excavated indicate a continuance of the ancient hunting, fishing, and gathering economy. The most significant feature of these sites, however, is that they do not represent temporary campsites, but "village settlements with fifteen to twenty permanent houses occupied at once. . ." (*ibid*). Kelly further notes that in the sites which he excavated in Fulton and Cobb Counties, there was little evidence of Hopewellian traits, except for numerous "bladelets" similar to those found at the Mandeville site to the south. He ends by saying that the Cartersville peoples lacked the sophistication seen at contemporary Hopewellian sites elsewhere in Georgia, but they had established village life without the food surplus of developed agriculture, which was once thought to be essential for the development of permanent villages (Kelly *op. cit.*:37).

One other apparently Hopewellian trait present in the Piedmont and mountains of Georgia consists of stone effigy mounds, stone piles, and stone or earth walls, embankments, and enclosures. Effigy mounds and earthworks are widely found in the Midwest in association with the Hopewell culture. As mentioned earlier in this chapter, some of the earthworks seem to be purely ceremonial in nature while others suggest defensive enclosures, particularly those situated on hilltops. In Georgia, perhaps the most widely known structure is the Rock Eagle effigy mound near Eatonton, Putnam County. Measuring 120 feet from wing tip to wing tip, and 102 feet from head to tail, this large bird effigy is constructed of quartzite stones of varying size. Another, lesser known, bird effigy is located a few miles away, and both show evidence of once having been enclosed by rings of the same quartzite (see Kelly 1954). Throughout the Piedmont, conical or rounded piles of quartzite stones are found and these are not to be confused with stonepiles resulting from modern field-clearing operations. Amateur archaeologists have reported finding the remains of burials underneath some of these small mounds, and there are reports of bird-effigy pipes having been found as well. However, archaeologists in Georgia have yet to find anything in unquestioned relationship to these constructions. A.R. Kelly, from the University of Georgia, conducted excavations in the breast area of the effigy at Rock Eagle. According to him, the team of archaeologists found a projectile point mixed in among the stones, and the remains of a cremated burial were found on the original ground surface underneath the effigy. The projectile point and the cremation may or may not have had any connection with the building of the effigy.

Stone or earth walls and embankments have been reported throughout northern Georgia. One of the most famous is the stone wall atop Fort Mountain in Murray County. This stone wall averages three to four feet in height, but in places it is as much as ten feet high. Width of the wall varies from four and a half feet to sixteen feet. In places, natural outcrops of boulders are incorporated into the wall. Here and there, the wall contains shallow holes or pits. This and other apparently prehistoric constructions were studied by Philip Smith in the 1950's. He records that the stone wall atop Fort Mountain is approximately 928 feet in length. Two test excavations yielded no artifacts (Smith 1956). Smith does not believe the wall to have been defensive, for he points out that its builders failed to make maximum use of natural topography, and indeed in some areas any defenders inside the wall would have been completely exposed to anyone approaching from outside the enclosure. Smith declares that this and other constructions are prehistoric, but does not speculate on their purpose.

Smith also investigated remains of this type in other parts of north Georgia, including a stone enclosure on Alec Mountain in Habersham County, and stone walls on Sand Mountain in Catoosa County, and on Rocky Face Mountain in Whitfield County. Other stone constructions were investigated near Kensington in Dade County, and on Mount Alto near Rome. He mentions the now-destroyed stone enclosures on Ladd Mountain in Bartow County and on Brown's Mount in Bibb County (Smith *op. cit.*). Similar structures in Alabama, Tennessee, and Kentucky are mentioned. A stone circle on a little knoll in Hall County was omitted by Smith, but is almost certainly related to the other quartzite mounds and enclosures described above. Smith's survey yielded no conclusive evidence of the time period during which these structures were probably built, but an excavation in south-central Tennessee did yield some clues.

Encircling an area of fifty acres, the earth and stone construction was investigated by archaeologists from the University of Tennessee in 1966. The investigations resulted in the finding of some features associated with the wall, and which contained charcoal. Radiocarbon dates obtained from these samples indicate construction of the walls at different times during the first three or four hundred years of the Christian era, i.e., A.D. 305, 220, and 430 (see Faulkner 1968). These dates compare favorably with dates from stone or earth hilltop enclosures in the Midwest associated with the Hopewell culture (*op. cit.*).

While not proven beyond any doubt, it is the opinion of archaeologists that the effigy mounds, stonepiles or cairns, and stone or earth walls and enclosures in Georgia and nearby states date from this same time and are thus related to Hopewell manifestations in the area. The nature of these monuments, whether ceremonial, secular, or both, will never be known.

In southern Georgia, one of the most widely known sites with Hopewellian affinities is the Mandeville site, now inundated by the Walter F. George Reservoir. Located in Clay County and excavated from 1959 through 1962, the site consisted of two earth mounds and a village area situated near the confluence of two small streams about a quarter mile from the Chattahoochee River (Kellar et al. 1962). Although it contained artifacts from several periods, the main occupation of the site, and the period of initial mound construction, falls during the period A.D. 140-500. Hopewellian traits were especially noticeable during the period A.D. 250-420. The archaeologists found that the first significant activity at the site was the establishment of a village, apparently covering the entire area later covered by Mound A, the larger of the two mounds. This occupation belonged to peoples assigned to the Deptford period of coastal and Coastal Plains prehistory and identifiable largely by their ceramics. Deptford ceramics, discussed more fully later in this chapter, are distinguished by their tetrapodal form and check or simple-stamped designs. Radiocarbon dates indicate that the construction of the burial mounds began about A.D. 250, and is marked by the presence of typically Hopewellian artifacts in the archaeological record.

Mound A measured approximately 240 by 170 feet, with an average height of fourteen feet. The mound summit was flat and this top layer had been added by later peoples. However, it was found that the mound had been flat-topped from its earliest stages of construction (Kellar et al. *op. cit.*:338). Initial stages of mound construction appear to date from late Deptford times. Middens in Mound A contained the remains of deer, bear, dog, opossum, fox squirrel, turkey, turtle, and gar (Smith 1979:181). Plant remains included charred hickory nut shell fragments. In the second stage of mound construction, Swift Creek pottery appears in the archaeological record and becomes the dominant type at this site.

Mound B was a dome-shaped burial mound one hundred feet in diameter and eighteen feet high. It was from burials in this mound that most of the Hopewellian artifacts were recovered, including a female figurine very like those found in Hopewell sites in Ohio. Also recovered here were copper ear-spools, pan pipes, galena, fragments of petrified wood, prismatic blades, and other objects (see photo 39 on page 80).

Swift Creek complicated-stamped pottery is an important type and apparently originated in southern Georgia (see photo 41 on page 81). It is present on some sites in north Georgia, as noted above, as well as in other states in the Southeast. Its affiliation with Hopewellian manifestations at the Mandeville site is very important, for identical ceramics are found at the Mann site in Posey County, Indiana, perhaps the largest Hopewell site anywhere (Kellar 1979). Swift Creek ceramics were first des-

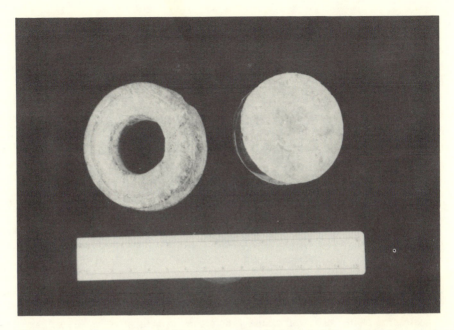

Copper ear-spools were worn in the ear lobes, after the lobes had been split and stretched. *(Dade County; from a private collection)* **Photo No. 42**

cribed by Kelly (1938) as a result of discoveries in excavations in central Georgia. Typical Swift Creek design elements have been described in the archaeological literature, and appear to have been executed by means of a carved wooden paddle. However, one fired clay stamp is known (see Milanich and Fairbanks (1980:120). The Swift Creek occupation at the Mandeville site began about A.D. 140 (Smith 1977:67). It was during this time that strong cultural ties developed between peoples living in southwest Georgia and those along the northwest Florida Gulf Coast. This is particularly reflected in the pottery, often called Santa Rosa-Swift Creek. Elsewhere in southern Georgia, Swift Creek ceramics have been found in association with burial mounds (see Smith *op. cit.*).

Eastward, along the Georgia coast and adjacent portions of the Coastal Plain, the Deptford culture existed about 500 B.C.-A.D. 600, and in this region it is believed to represent "a coastal-dwelling population whose subsistence centered on the exploitation of coastal resources such as fish, shellfish, deer, plants and other wild foods" (Milanich and Fairbanks 1980:66). Milanich (1972:27) sees the Deptford culture as representing a period of transition from the hunting and gathering of small bands to the establishment of the permanent villages associated with plant cultivation and the complex ceremonialism of later times. As evidence of this transition, he points to excavations on Cumberland Island which revealed that early Deptford sites were composed of five to ten house structures, while later villages contained as many as twenty-five structures. The presence of such substantial structures suggests long-term residence during a part of the year, and this probably means that the same group lived at the same site on a seasonal basis year after year. Archaeological surveys indicate that such villages were found along the coast about every eight to ten miles on Cumberland Island and the Florida Gulf Coast (Milanich *op. cit.*:27-28). The idea of the coastal orientation of Deptford peoples is based on several things.

Deptford remains are found along the Georgia coast and the Florida Gulf Coast. Because of the rise in sea level since 1000 B.C., it is believed that many Deptford sites are now underwater. Those sites that are known, however, point to intensive exploitation of coastal resources, both marine and land. Coastal Deptford sites appear as shell middens. Some of these shell deposits are in the form of piles of mainly oyster shells, seemingly accumulated as refuse heaps adjacent to house structures. In other instances, these deposits overlap, forming rather large linear deposits (Milanich 1980), but large deposits from this period are rare on the southern coast of Georgia (Cook 1977). According to Milanich's study (*ibid.*), Deptford sites are located on live oak-magnolia hammocks on the mainland and in the barrier islands, and adjacent to the saltwater marsh. From such locations, the people could exploit the plentiful resources found nearby. Faunal remains, including those of deer, raccoon, opossum, West Indian seal, various species of turtle, and various species of saltwater fish furnish evidence of their subsistence. No evidence for domesticated plants has been found in a Deptford context in this region, and other plant remains are extremely rare, but Milanich (*op. cit.*) speculates that wild nuts, fruits, and tubers formed a substantial part of the diet. Presumably, the abundance of food in the coastal environment, and the efficiency with which Deptford peoples exploited it, gave rise to larger populations and larger, more permanent villages. In addition, Deptford sites along the rivers inland in the Coastal Plain possibly indicate short-term seasonal exploitation of inland food sources (see Milanich and Fairbanks *op. cit.*:72).

We know little about the types of tools used by Deptford peoples. We do know that they worked with wood, for designs were applied to their pottery by means of carved wooden paddles. Also, triangular stone projectile points have occasionally been found on Deptford sites, but whether these were used with a bow and arrow or atl-atl is not known (Milanich and Fairbanks *op. cit.*:76). Net and basketry impressions have been noticed on some Deptford pottery, giving rise to speculations about their use of nets and basketry weirs for procuring fish (*ibid.*). However, this must remain speculation, for there is no direct information on how fish or other marine resources were obtained. Additionally, no bone fishhooks have been found on Deptford sites. Other artifacts include shell tools (picks, hammers, gouges, and chisels), hammerstones, pottery abraders, and grinding stones (Milanich 1980:176).

While archaeologists know very little about how Deptford peoples killed, caught, trapped, or collected their food, we do know more about other aspects of life. Some entire house structures have been excavated, providing valuable information on Deptford peoples and how they lived. Excavations on Cumberland Island revealed what Milanich (1980:175) interprets as a winter house. It was oval-shaped, approximately thirty by twenty feet, with openings at one end and on one side. A large hearth dominated the portion of the structure nearest the openings, which was separated from the rest of the structure by a small partition. Exterior walls were anchored in wall trenches. A second structure, thought to represent a summer dwelling, measured approximately thirteen by twenty feet and evidently was open-sided like the chickees of modern Seminole Indians. Piles of shells had accumulated near the remains of both structures (Milanich *op. cit.*).

On St. Catherine's Island, several sand burial mounds have been excavated and are believed to be associated with the Deptford occupation. Several of the mounds yielded radiocarbon dates which lead archaeologists to believe that these particular mounds were constructed about A.D. 125 (Thomas and Larsen 1979:143). Other mounds apparently were constructed about A.D. 570. No Hopewellian artifacts are known from these and other Deptford mounds, but possibly the idea of mound-building diffused to Deptford peoples. However, they were never absorbed into or heavily influenced by the Hopewellian system.

Late Woodland times are distinguishable in virtually all parts of the state by ceramic styles, for the basic lifeway apparently was unchanged. In northern Georgia, late Swift Creek ceramics are found on some sites, but are not common (see Campbell and Weed 1984:27). Indeed, no late Woodland sites were found in the survey of the Richard B. Russell reservoir (Taylor and Smith 1978; Campbell and Weed *op. cit.*). This situation is interpreted as indicating a continuation of earlier ceramic decorative styles without the introduction of other types, and is not thought to represent abandonment of the area by its human inhabitants. Ceramics decorated in the style known as Napier are found on sites scattered throughout northern Georgia, and are thought to have given rise to ceramic styles of the early Mississippian period in this part of the state (see Chapter 6).

Perhaps the largest and best-known Late Woodland site in Georgia is the Kolomoki site in Early County. The site is located on Kolomoki Creek about six miles from its confluence with the Chattahoochee River and covers some three hundred acres. The

Potsherds decorated in the Napier complicated stamp design. *(Banks County; from a private collection)* Photo No. 43

central area is dominated by a large temple mound, measuring 325 by 200 feet at the base and 56 feet in height. A large plaza area was immediately in front of the mound, and a village surrounded the plaza. Eight other mounds, one of which may not be prehistoric, are located on the site (Sears 1956). Excavation of these mounds revealed burials, primarily in two of the smaller mounds, and evidence of platforms or other type structures in some of the other mounds. Mound E yielded fifty-four complete pottery vessels, all of which had been placed on the ground surface and the whole area of the mound then covered in a cap of red clay.

Some of the most unusual artifacts recovered at the Kolomoki site are the effigy vessels. These were often made in the shape of birds or animals and contained pre-cut holes as part of the over-all design. Most of these vessels could have had no utilitarian value, and so they are regarded by archaeologists as being ceremonial in nature. On the other hand, utilitarian pottery was also recovered from this site, and much of it has been classified as a late Swift Creek ware.

The Swift Creek settlement of the Kolomoki site dates from about A.D. 800 and site occupation extended into the succeeding time period, the Mississippian. Apparently, the site was abandoned about A.D. 1300. Kolomoki was obviously the center of great political and ceremonial activity in this region of Georgia and adjacent states, and seems to have been part of a larger ceremonial complex called Weeden Island. Milanich and Fairbanks (*op. cit.*:91) point out that Weeden Island refers to "several distinct, regional cultures . . . that shared the same basic ceremonial complex." The socio-political implications of Kolomoki in regional prehistory are discussed more fully in Sears (1956), Milanich and Fairbanks (*op. cit.*), Smith (1977), and Steinen (1977).

The cultural chronology of the Georgia coast is marked in Late Woodland times by the introduction of ceramics decorated by cord marks. This is called Wilmington cordmarked pottery and was introduced about A.D. 600, for it immediately follows Deptford ceramics in the archaeological record. Caldwell and others regard cordmarking as a trait introduced from north of the area and is thus not directly related to the cordmarked ceramics of inland portions of Georgia of the Early Woodland. Along the lower Georgia coast, an intervening phase between Deptford and Wilmington has been identified. Called the Kelvin phase, it is thought to date from A.D. 600-900 and is distinguished by ceramic difference and mortuary customs which are divergent from those of the northern coastal area (see Cook 1979).

Summary

It has been noted in this chapter that the basic way of life for peoples living in what is now Georgia changed but little from the Archaic to the Woodland period. In fact, some tool types typically associated with the Archaic continued to be made into early Woodland times. Changes are seen, however, in the method of manufacture and decoration of pottery. The Woodland, beginning about 1000 B.C., saw the beginning of the rope-coil method of pottery manufacture, the use of grit or sand as the tempering medium, and the introduction of design elements executed by means of a carved

Cord-marked pottery from the Georgia coast. *(Liberty County; from a private collection)*
Photo No. 44

wooden paddle or a cord-wrapped stick. In time, patterns of decoration changed as popularity of certain design elements waxed and waned.

It was also during the Woodland period that peoples in Georgia began to be influenced by the Hopewell culture, centered in the Ohio Valley. This influence is apparently manifested through the spread of a religion or ceremonial activity which involved the construction of burial mounds, the use of certain objects (pan pipes, mica cutouts, platform or effigy pipes, etc.), and the construction of effigy mounds and stone or earth walls, embankments, and "fortifications." Possibly this ceremonialism spread through trade networks, for the Ohio Valley Hopewell centers contain artifacts made of exotic goods from locations hundreds of miles away. Specifically, mica and possibly some copper was obtained from the Southern Appalachians, including north Georgia, and conch shells were obtained from the Gulf Coast. It is very likely that the Chattahoochee River functioned as a major artery in this trade network, for it is near the Chattahoochee that the Mandeville site arose. In northwest Georgia, presumably on the route to the Ohio Valley, the Tunacunnhee site was situated.

With the widespread use of pottery, there are certain changes apparent in Woodland subsistence as revealed in site surveys and excavations. Apparently, the boiling of food in ceramic containers meant that more calories were made available than was the case with roasting or stone-boiling (see Munson 1976; Crook 1984). This meant that Woodland peoples could derive greater food value from resources than was previously the case. Therefore, villages or base camps were situated in the riverbottoms and thus nearest to the most abundant resources. Temporary camps were established seasonally in other areas where hunting and the gathering of certain resources took place. Thus, Woodland sites are not common in upland situations, while villages or

A bird-effigy pipe, possibly representing the now extinct Carolina parakeet. *(Hall County; from a private collection)* Photo No. 45

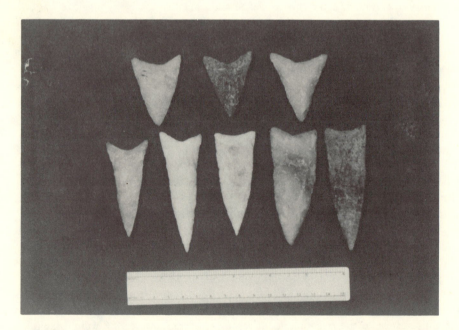

Further examples of Woodland projectile points. *(Union County; from a private collection)* Photo No. 46

base camp sites are fairly common in the riverbottoms. Along the coast, the sites occur mostly in the live oak/magnolia hammocks near the saltwater marsh, with all its bird, animal, fish, and shellfish resources.

The increased residential stability, and apparently a population increase in late Woodland times, sets the stage for the large populations and the agricultural economic base of the next time period, the Mississippian.

REFERENCES: CHAPTER V

Bowen, William R., *Archaeological Investigations at 9CK(DOT)7, Cherokee County, Georgia,*
1982   Occasional Papers in Cultural Resource Management No. 1, Georgia Department of Transportation, Office of Environmental Analysis, Atlanta.

Caldwell, Joseph R., "Trend and Tradition in the Prehistory of the Eastern United States," *American Anthropological Association Memoir No. 88.*
1958

_____, "Survey and Excavations in the Allatoona Reservoir, Northern
n.d.   Georgia," Unpublished manuscript, Department of Anthropology, University of Georgia, Athens.

Campbell, L. Janice, and Carol S. Weed, eds., *The Beaverdam Group: Archaeological Investigations*
1984   *at 9EB92, 9EB207, 9EB208, and 9EB219, Richard B. Russell Multiple Resource Area, Elbert County, Georgia,* Russell Papers, Archaeological Services, Atlanta.

Cook, Fred C., "The Lower Georgia Coast as a Cultural Sub-Region," *Early Georgia,* Vol. 5, No.
1977   1-2, pp. 15-36.

_____, "Kelvin: A Late Woodland Phase on the Southern Georgia Coast,"
1979   *Early Georgia,* Vol. 7, No. 2, pp. 65-86.

Crook, Morgan R., Jr., *Cagle Site Report: Archaic and Early Woodland Period Manifestations in*
1984   *the North Georgia Piedmont,* Occasional Papers in Cultural Resource Management No. 2, Georgia Department of Transportation, Office of Environmental Analysis, Atlanta.

DePratter, Chester B., "The Refuge Phase on the Coastal Plain of Georgia," *Early Georgia,* Vol. 4,
1976   pp. 1-13.

_____, "Ceramics," in *The Anthropology of St. Catherines Island 2: The*
1979   *Refuge-Deptford Mortuary Complex,* Ed. by David Hurst Thomas and Clark Spencer Larsen, Anthropological Papers of the American Museum of Natural History, Vol. 56, Part I, pp. 109-131.

Faulkner, Charles H., *The Old Stone Fort,* University of Tennessee Press, Knoxville.
1968

Ferguson, Leland G., "Prehistoric Mica Mines in the Southern Appalachians," *South Carolina*
1974   *Antiquities,* Vol. 2, Journal of the Archaeological Society of South Carolina, Columbia, pp. 211-217.

Garrow, Patrick H., "The Woodland Period North of the Fall Line," *Early Georgia,* Vol. 3, No. 1,
1975   pp. 17-26.

Jefferies, Richard W., *The Tunacunnhee Site: Evidence of Hopewell Interaction in Northwest*
1976   *Georgia,* Anthropological Papers of the University of Georgia, No. 1, Athens.

Kellar, James H., A.R. Kelly, and Edward V. McMichael. "The Mandeville Site in Southwest Geor-
1962   gia," *American Antiquity,* Vol. 27, No. 3, pp. 336-355.

_____, "The Mann Site and "Hopewell" in the Lower Wabash-Ohio
1979   Valley," in *Hopewell Archaeology: The Chillicothe Conference,* Ed. by David S. Brose and N'omi Greber, Kent State University Press, Kent, Ohio, pp. 100-107.

Kelly, A.R., *A Preliminary Report on Archaeological Explorations at Macon, Georgia,* Bureau of
1938   American Ethnology, Bulletin 119, pp. 1-69.

_____, "The Eatonton Effigy Eagle Mounds and Related Stone Structures
1954   in Putnam County, Georgia," *Georgia Mineral Newsletter,* Vol. VII, No. 2, Atlanta, pp. 82-86.

_____, "Early Villages on the Chattahoochee River, Georgia," *Archaeology,*
1973   Vol. 26, No. 1, pp. 32-37.

Lepionka, Larry, "The Early Woodland Ceramic Typology of the Second Refuge Site, Jasper
1983   County, South Carolina," *South Carolina Antiquities,* Vol. 15, Nos. 1-2, Archaeological
Society of South Carolina, Columbia, pp. 17-30.

Milanich, Jerald T., and Charles H. Fairbanks, *Florida Archaeology,* Academic Press, Inc., New
1980   York.

_____, "The Deptford Phase: An adaptation of Hunting-Gathering Bands
1972   to the Southeastern Coastal Strand," *Southeastern Archaeological Conference, Bulletin No.
15,* Ed. by Bettye J. Broyles, Morgantown, West Virginia, pp. 21-23.

_____, "Coastal Georgia Deptford Culture: Growth of a Concept," in
1980   *Excursions in Southeastern Geology: The Archaeology-Geology of the Georgia Coast,* Ed.
by James D. Howard, Chester B. DePratter, and Robert W. Frey, Guidebook No. 20, Georgia Geologic Survey, Environmental Protection Division, Department of Natural Resources,
Atlanta, pp. 170-178.

Munson, Patrick J., "Changes in and Relationships of Subsistence, Settlement, and Population in
1976   the Central Illinois River Valley," Paper presented at the 41st Annual Meeting of the Society for American Archaeology, St. Louis, Missouri, May 6-8.

Sears, William H., *Excavations at Kolomoki: Final Report,* University of Georgia Series in Anthro-
1956   pology, No. 5, University of Georgia Press, Athens.

Smith, Betty A., "Southwest Georgia Prehistory: An Overview," *Early Georgia,* Vol. 5, Nos. 1-2,
1977   pp. 61-72.

_____, "The Hopewell Connection in Southwest Georgia," in *Hopewell*
1979   *Archaeology: The Chillocothe Conference,* Ed. by David S. Brose and N'omi Greber, Kent
State University Press, Kent, Ohio, pp. 181-187.

Smith, Philip E., "Aboriginal Stone Constructions in the Southern Piedmont," *University of*
1962   *Georgia Laboratory of Archaeology Series, No. 4, Part 2,* Athens.

Steinen, Karl, "Weeden Island in Southwest Georgia," *Early Georgia,* Vol. 5, Nos. 1-2, pp. 73-87.
1977

Taylor, Richard L., and Marion F. Smith, *The Report of the Intensive Survey of the Richard B.*
1978   *Russell Dam and Lake, Savannah River, Georgia and South Carolina,* Research Manuscript
Series 142, Institute of Archaeology and Anthropology, University of South Carolina,
Columbia.

Thomas, David Hurst, and Clark Spencer Larsen, *The Anthropology of St. Catherines Island 2:*
1979   *The Refuge-Deptford Mortuary Complex,* Anthropological Papers of the American Museum
of Natural History, Vol. 56, Part 1, New York.

Wauchope, Robert, *Archaeological Survey of Northern Georgia,* Memoirs of the Society for Ameri-
1966   can Archaeology, No. 21, Salt Lake City.

Willey, Gordon R., *An Introduction to American Archaeology, Vol. 1: North and Middle America,*
1966   Prentice-Hall, Inc., Englewood Cliffs, New Jersey.

Williams, Stephen, Ed., *The Waring Papers: The Southern Cult, and Other Archaeological Essays,*
1968   by Antonio J. Waring, Jr., University of Georgia Press, Athens.

Chapter VI

THE MISSISSIPPIAN
A.D. 1000–1500

*T*he Mississippian period represents a marked break from the past in many respects. Numerous authors have interpreted the appearance of Mississippian sites, marked by flat-topped earth mounds, palisades, and other features as representing a movement of people into the area, bringing with them Mississippian cultural patterns. The earlier sites do indeed seem to be outposts, surrounded by peoples pursuing a Woodland lifeway, but eventually the Mississippian way of life spread to virtually all peoples in the Southeast. This way of life was one with agriculture as the economic base, with hunting, gathering, and fishing remaining important, but secondary, activities. There was an elaborate ceremonialism, too, and art motifs, artifacts, and apparent practices inherent in this religion are virtually the same at ceremonial centers from Oklahoma to North Carolina. Certainly, we are not dealing here with one tribe of people, but several tribes following the same agricultural way of life and participating in the same ceremonial complex. In Georgia, sites of this period are found statewide, with some of the largest and most impostant Mississippian sites in the Southeast being situated in the northern and central portions of the state.

Evidence of the intrusion of a group of people into Georgia, and with them the establishment of the economic and ceremonial complex identified as Mississippian, is seen at some sites near Macon, dating from about A.D. 1000. Excavations at the large ceremonial site now preserved in the Ocmulgee National Monument began in 1933 as part of the Civil Works Administration activities. A.R. Kelly was the archaeologist in charge of excavations here and at other sites in the immediate area, where excavations were carried out through 1938. One of the first excavations was at Mound C, subsequently named the Funeral Mound, which had been partially destroyed by railroad construction. The archaeologists learned that the mound had been constructed in seven phases (Fairbanks 1956:24). Apparently, each phase had to do with a ceremony, for there is evidence here and at other Mississippian mounds that the temple atop the mound was burned. A new layer of earth was then applied to the entire mound, and a new temple was constructed on the summit. From time to time, individuals were buried in the mound, and because they were buried here and often exotic goods were placed with them, archaeologists believe that these represent the elite of Mississippian society, very probably members of the priestly families (see photo 51 on page 102).

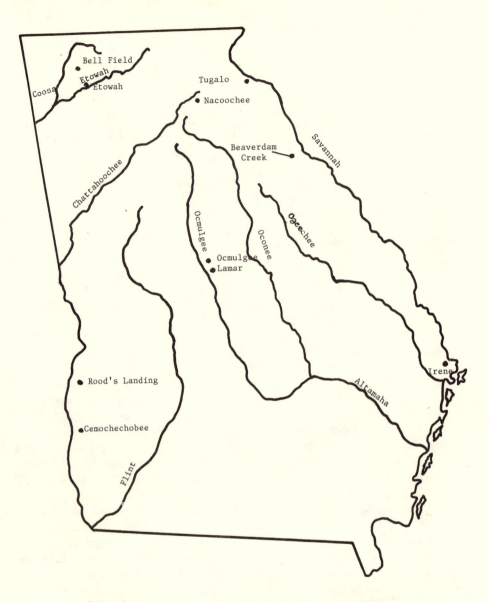

Some of the more important Mississippian sites in Georgia. Map 6

This and all other mounds were constructed entirely by human labor and without the use of wheeled or other vehicles. Dirt was brought a basket-load at a time, and by the coloration of the soil, these individual basketloads can often be distinguished in the course of excavating a mound. Archaeologists discovered steps on the side of the first or original mound stage at the Funeral Mound. Extending from the base to the summit, the steps were made of a brilliant red clay placed in horizontal rows on the blue-gray clay of the mound. The steps were heavily worn by the trodding of feet (Kelly 1938; Fairbanks *op. cit.*:25). Of the numerous burials discovered in Mound C, one of the most interesting was certainly the tomb of a very important person. The grave pit was eight feet long, and of the skeletal material, only a femur was preserved. But the grave goods were astonishing. Two copper plates, evidently representing the sun and its rays, and two copper-covered, cut puma jaws were included in the burial goods. The copper salts had preserved fragments of cane matting and a piece of twisted cord (Fairbanks *op. cit.*). The copper-covered puma jaws may very possibly be related to an Indian legend given in Fairbanks (p. 46) in which it is recounted how the Creeks managed to kill such a beast that had preyed upon them. Afterwards, they kept some of his bones and used them in a ceremonial fashion.

It is difficult to isolate any one aspect of the excavations on the Macon Plateau as "the most important," for all were of primary importance in understanding the prehistory of central Georgia. But certainly the most unique finding was that of the ceremonial earth lodge. When workers began excavating a small mound some three feet high and seventy feet in diameter, they discovered a red clay wall surrounding an inner area forty-two feet in diameter. This clay buttress "surrounded the clay floor so as to give the building the appearance of being semi-subterranean, although it was actually entirely above ground" (Fairbanks 1946:95). A circular fire basin some four feet in diameter was found just south of the center of the structure, and a compact layer of ash still remained at the bottom of the pit. Further excavations revealed an entrance passageway some twenty-six feet long and some two feet wide. This entrance passageway was lined with the charred remains of split posts, behind which was found charred remains of split-cane matting.

Inside the structure, and directly opposite the entrance was a "large, packed clay platform shaped to represent an eagle" (Fairbanks *op. cit.*). This platform was sixteen feet long, fourteen feet wide, and nine to twelve inches high. A shallow groove marked the beak, slight grooves on the shoulders apparently represented feathers, and the eye was indicated by the "forked eye" motif. Three shallow depressions were located near the wall, and "on either side of the platform and extending around the wall to the entrance was a series of seats, twenty-three on the northerly and twenty four on the southerly side of the lodge" (*ibid.*). These seats were modeled on a clay bench, and each had an oval depression directly in front of it. The roof was supported primarily by four large posts, the charred remains of which were intact. Numerous pieces of charred timbers littered the floor of the structure, and underneath these timbers was a layer of earth containing fragments of charred cane. The charred roof timbers were found in a radiating pattern around the fire basin. These and other charred remains obviously represent debris from a burned roof. This roof had originally been covered with a layer of earth and cane, which had apparently fallen in before the supporting timbers collapsed. Botanical studies revealed that the roof timbers were some species of pine, while the huge support posts were a variety of oak. This earth lodge, radiocarbon dated to A.D. 1000 (Wilson 1964:202), was reconstructed and is now a popular attraction at the Ocmulgee National Monument.

A view of the mounds at Ocmulgee National Monument. *(Courtesy National Park Service, Ocmul-*

gee National Monument) **Photo No. 47**

A stage in the excavation of a mound at Ocmulgee National Monument. *(Courtesy National Park Service, Ocmulgee National Monument)* **Photo No. 48**

A view of the interior of the restored ceremonial lodge, showing the fire pit and the eagle effigy modeled in red clay. *(Courtesy National Park Service, Ocmulgee National Monument)* **Photo No. 49**

Near this earth lodge was Mound D, named the Cornfield Mound because excavation revealed that the mound had been constructed directly on a cornfield. In fact, the corn rows, and even a path through the field, were preserved. At Mound A, the remains of several superimposed buildings were found, and the partially obliterated remains of another earth lodge were discovered several hundred feet west of the earth lodge described above. Still another such structure was found in excavations at Brown's Mount, some five miles from the Macon Plateau.

Pottery associated with the early Mississippian occupation of the Macon Plateau is almost all categorized as Bibb Plain, characterized by a plain globular vessel tempered with grit and/or crushed mussel shell. Some pottery has a red film, but otherwise is mostly undecorated. Clay pipe fragments were also found, but were not numerous.

Since bone was only rarely preserved, and modern recovery techniques for small seeds, etc. were unknown, little indication was found relating to the subsistence of the Mississippian peoples living on the Macon Plateau. The cornfield underneath Mound D was perhaps the best find in this regard, and it demonstrates the agricultural nature of the economy.

Excavations at the Cornfield Mound, showing the remains of rows in the field over which the mound was constructed. *(Courtesy National Park Service, Ocmulgee National Monument)* Photo No. 50

In further excavations on the Macon Plateau, archaeologists discovered that the ceremonial earth lodge and nearby mound had been at least partially enclosed by a ditch, presumed to have been for defensive purposes. Such fortifications are typical of early Mississippian sites here and elsewhere in the Southeast, and indeed moats and palisades remained a feature of important ceremonial centers throughout the period. The remains of such a fortification were found in excavations in the Allatoona reservoir associated with the early Mississippian Woodstock phase in this part of the state. The site of the fortification and village complex was located on the Etowah River at Proctor's Bend (see Caldwell 1950). The ceramics associated with this phase are decorated by stamped designs consisting of barred lozenges or nested diamonds. This ceramic style is widely recognized as representing the earliest Mississippian cultures in northern Georgia. The village at this site was surrounded by a shallow ditch, with two lines of palisades just inside the ditch. Towers had been set at intervals along the palisade, as indicated by the post-hole pattern. Apparently, the pattern of small villages enclosed by a palisade is typical of the Woodstock phase, despite the fact that only one Woodstock site is known to have contained a temple mound (Taylor and Smith 1978:108). Charred maize kernels were found in a pit associated with the Woodstock phase at the Stamp Creek site, also in the Allatoona reservoir, and this attests to maize agriculture in this part of the state at this time.

Following Woodstock in northern Georgia, are the Etowah phases, subdivided according to a sequence of ceramic decorations. Etowah sites often include large villages, fortifications, and temple mounds. The best-known site of this era is the Etowah site itself, near Cartersville, Bartow County. This huge complex originally covered some fifty-two acres and consisted of seven mounds and a plaza surrounded by a moat and palisade. The village area occupied the riverbottoms surrounding the ceremonial area. The site has long been the object of curiosity and has received the attention of numerous archaeologists. However, the first serious attempt to learn about the Etowah site was that of Warren K. Moorehead.

Moorehead was from the Phillips Academy, Andover, Massachusetts, and began operations at Etowah in 1925. His primary attention was given to Mound C, which had already been partially explored by Rogan of the Bureau of American Ethnology. Moorehead's report, first publicized in 1932, was reprinted in 1979 (Moorehead 1979) and represents the most complete description of work at the Etowah site, despite numerous excavations since his time. No report of the archaeological excavations in Mound C conducted by the University of Georgia and the Georgia Historical Commission during the 1950's has yet appeared, and but few articles provide any insight into what was discovered in these and other more recent excavations. The following discussion represents a brief overview of the archaeology of the Etowah site gleaned from the published works.

The ceremonial center itself consisted originally of seven mounds and a plaza area, surrounded by a moat and palisade. In the course of more than a hundred years of intensive farming, four of the smaller mounds have been completely obliterated and portions of the moat have been filled in. The entire site is dominated by Mound A, which measures some 380 feet by 330 feet at the base and is a little over 60 feet high at present. This large mound was visited by Rev. Elias Cornelius, in the company of several Indian leaders, in the early 1800's. He described it as follows in an article first published in 1819:

".... judging from the degree of its declivity, the *perpendicular height* cannot be less than seventy-five feet .... Its top is level, and at the time I visited it, was so completely covered with weeds, bushes, and trees of most luxuriant growth, that I could not examine it as well as I wished. Its diameter, I judged, must be one hundred and fifty feet."

(Rev. Elias Cornelius as quoted in Wauchope 1966:251-2.)

Mound A has never been excavated. Because the former landowners raised crops on the mound summit, it is estimated that some ten to fifteen feet of the uppor portion of the mound has been lost. In the 1970's, an archaeological team from Georgia State University conducted excavations on the present mound summit, but the results of this work remain unpublished.

Of the two other structures, Mound B and Mound C, only the latter has been completely excavated. Mound C was investigated by various researchers in the latter nineteenth century, but serious excavations began in 1925 with Moorehead's work. Moorehead discovered over one hundred burials, several of which contained elaborate articles now known to be associated with the so-called Southern Cult, discussed later in this chapter. In one such burial, workers discovered a copper-covered wooden cup or object, with a coiled serpent carved in relief. Scales of copper still adhered to the surface in some places (see Moorehead pp. 68-9). In this same burial was found a finely made flint blade 26¼ inches long. The graves containing such elaborate goods were generally capped by flat slabs of stone and often contained large numbers of shell beads.

Most of the archaeological knowledge of Mound C comes from the few published articles resulting from the excavations of the 1950's under the auspices of the Georgia Historical Commission. Earlier reports are lacking in detail, and indeed excavation procedures had not developed to the extent that they could be called archaeology in the contemporary sense. Mound C was approximately 150 feet square at the base and probably 60 feet square at the summit. Although previous excavations, floods, etc. had removed much of the structure, Larson (1971:58) estimates its original height as about eighteen feet. The mound had been constructed in five phases, each phase being marked by the addition of a new layer of clay over the whole structure and (probably) the construction of a new building on the summit. The base of the mound was encircled by a log palisade, and in later stages of mound construction, numerous burials were placed just inside the palisade and around the base of the mound. Larson's article deals with a discussion of the burials associated with the final phase of mound construction (*op. cit.*). All were found in square or rectangular pits, and most contained the remains of a single individual. These burials were associated with the Wilbanks ceramic period, discussed later in this chapter. Radiocarbon dates place the burials between A.D. 1000 and 1400.

Males and females representing a wide range of ages were interred in Mound C, and this final phase of burials contained the so-called Southern Cult materials. It is noted that not all burials contained grave goods, but where such artifacts were present, nearly all were ornaments from a costume or were ceremonial "weapons." Ornaments included various kinds of ear ornaments (most were discs of wood covered with sheet

An excavated log tomb burial at Ocmulgee. *(Courtesy National Park Service, Ocmulgee National Monument)* Photo No. 51

copper); engraved shell gorgets; pendants and necklaces of massive shell beads; wooden beads covered with sheet copper; beaded chokers and beaded bands worn on the arm and legs; headdresses and hair ornaments; cutouts of copper; sea turtle shell; mica cutouts apparently attached to garments; and rattles in the shape of discs or animals carved of wood, covered with sheet copper, and containing a cavity with small gravel

Mound B at the Etowah site. *(Courtesy Georgia Department of Natural Resources)* **Photo No. 52**

placed inside. Most of the rattles appear to have been attached to the ankles, but one hand-held example was found (Larson *op. cit.*:62-3).

In addition, various kinds of axes and long chipped stone blades were found. Copper celts, stone celts, copper-covered stone celts, spatulate stone celts, and monolithic axes were all found in burials, and Larson (*ibid.*) maintains that none could have been used as an actual tool or weapon. Thus, the interpretation of their ceremonial nature.

Pottery was not commonly found in burials at Mound C. Most of the vessels that were found were decorated in the Wilbanks complicated stamped design, which followed the Etowah ceramic types in north Georgia, and represent utilitarian ware. Other objects found among the grave goods included shell bowls, most made from *Busycon* species, and stone paint palettes. These palettes were found lying face down over several pieces of mineral pigment, including ocher, kaolin, graphite, and galena. All were locally available.

In addition to the burials placed in simple rectangular pits, some had been interred in log tombs. Concerning the latter, Kelly and Larson (1954) described an unusual burial in the following manner:

"One of the most remarkable of the log tombs was Burial No. 38, on the north side of the mound. The pit was some ten feet square, with forty-two small posts set upright in a wall trench around the edge of the pit floor. The logs forming the roof had collapsed and were lying on the floor, covered by the clay overburden. Arranged on the floor were five skeletons, each accompanied by a copper celt with part of the wooden handle preserved. A polished

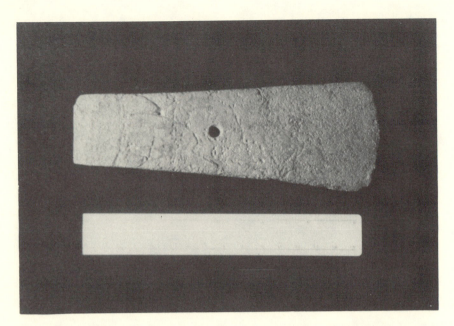

A copper celt. *(Murray County; from a private collection)* **Photo No. 53**

stone disc with a scalloped edge (ten inches in diameter) lay near one skull. A lump of graphite and a lump of galena (lead ore) found under the disc showed that it must have served as a palette for the preparation of face or body paint. With each skull were the remains of an elaborate headdress formed of pieces of copper cut out and embossed. Copper-covered wooden beads set with seed pearls were also found, as well as a conch-shell gorget bearing an excised cross design, fragments of split cane matting, numerous shell beads and a large conch shell."

(from Kelly and Larson 1954.)

Larson (1971; 1959) discusses the headdresses in more detail. He says that each individual in this burial was accompanied by an elaborate headdress "composed of small embossed sheet copper ornaments and hawk skins as well as other feathers" (1971.65). The copper ornaments were attached to small wooden rods several inches in length, and these apparently were attached to a leather cap or band in a fan-like arrangement (Larson 1959). He goes on to state that no two headdresses were alike, and that some of the copper ornaments retained the impressions of feathers, indicating that some of the headdresses had feathers attached to the framework. One such headdress has been reconstructed and is on display at the Etowah Museum.

Another important find in Mound C is described by Kelly and Larson (*op. cit.*):

"In another log tomb we encountered what is perhaps our most important single find. Associated with the remains of three dismembered bodies were two large marble figures, one representing a man, the other a woman. Each stands two feet high and weighs close to one hundred pounds . . . The woman

THIS REPLICA IS AN ARTICLE OF
CULT COSTUME. THERE IS DETAILED
DATA FOR THE RECONSTRUCTION,
THE MOST POPULAR OF MANY TYPES.
THE COPPER SYMBOLS & OTHER
EVIDENCE OF FINERY WERE TAKEN
FROM GRAVES OF PRIESTS.

The reconstructed headdress exhibited in the museum at the Etowah site. *(Courtesy Georgia Department of Natural Resources)* **Photo No. 54**

is represented as kneeling, with hands on knees. She wears a skirt with a belt. She has a flat, disc-shaped headdress and a knapsack-like object on her back. The man, a larger figure, is seated cross-legged, with hands on knees. His curious headdress includes a coil or bunch (of hair?) on the back of the head. On both figures the ears are painted red, the eyes white with black pupils, and other details are greenish black, carbon black, red or white. Both figures are well carved and polished, with details carefully rendered. Their rather stiff and bulky appearance lacks the grace and fluid lines of the human figures represented on the embossed copper plates and gorgets from Etowah."

(Kelly and Larson 1954).

Larson later added that the floor of the tomb was in complete disarray and that the stone effigies had apparently been broken accidentally when one was dropped on the other.

Several similar stone effigies have been found at the Etowah site over the years. Moorehead found an effigy placed in a small stone-lined grave in Mound C. There are early historic descriptions of similar stone statues seen by explorers in temples on the summit of mounds in some parts of the Southeast. According to their statements, the statues were viewed by the Indians as images of a god and were held in awe and reverence (see Moorehead *op. cit.*:27).

The marble effigies from Mound C at Etowah, front view. *(Courtesy Georgia Department of Natural Resources)* Photo No. 55

The marble effigies from Mound C at Etowah, side view. *(Courtesy Georgia Department of Natural Resources)* Photo No. 56

It is obvious that Mound C at Etowah was the burial place of an elite group in Etowah society. Because men, women, and children of all ages were buried here, Larson (1971) suggests that the graves represent those of a family, most likely the family or descent group furnishing political and ceremonial leadership in Etowah society.

Surrounding the ceremonial center, the village area at the Etowah site spread over the riverbottoms. The village area is not nearly as attractive as the mounds, with their elaborate remains, and so the dwellings of the ordinary citizens have received less attention from archaeologists. Limited excavations have been carried out, however, and these have revealed that burials in the village area are rarely accompanied by grave goods. Occasionally, a stone celt, a pottery vessel, or a shell gorget is found, but little else. Houses, as defined by postmoulds and other remains, were wattle and daub structures, square, round, or rectangular, with a fire pit.

Not all the villages of this time were located around the large ceremonial centers. Indeed, most Mississippian sites lack mounds. Studies of the river system in the area of the Etowah site have revealed that all up and down the Etowah River and its tributaries are Mississippian sites. Some contain small temple mounds and were probably ceremonial centers subsidiary to the main Etowah site. Others do not contain mounds and are evidently the remains of small villages. Situated on tributary creeks and streams, generally in small bottomlands, are sites identified as the remains of hamlets or individual dwellings. Throughout northern Georgia, this is the basic pattern of the Mississippian settlement system.

An engraved shell gorget. *(Murray County; from a private collection)* **Photo No. 57**

In the eastern Piedmont along the Savannah River, there are a few Mississippian village sites with mounds. In his survey of the Hartwell reservoir, Caldwell (1974) found a village site with a mound located about every nine miles along the Tugalo River. Farther south, he investigated the Rembert Mounds (Caldwell 1953) in Elbert County, and more recently the Beaverdam Creek Mound, also in Elbert County, has been explored (Lee 1976; Rudolph and Hally 1984). The pottery associated with the Mississippian period along the Savannah River is identified as primarily Savannah-Wilbanks. The most common designs stamped on the vessels are concentric circles, filfot crosses, and multiline figures-of-eight (Taylor and Smith 1978:108).

Below the Fall Line in Georgia, Mississippian sites with mounds are less numerous and are found mostly along the Chattahoochee, Ocmulgee, and Savannah Rivers. Ceramics of the early Mississippian period in much of south Georgia are closely related to the Weeden Island ceramic tradition in Florida. The Kolomoki site, previously discussed, is one of the largest known sites of this time and appears to span late Woodland-early Mississippian times. Also in west Georgia, Caldwell investigated the Rood's Landing site, a large Mississippian site with eight mounds and associated plaza areas in Stewart County (Caldwell 1955). More recently, an earth lodge associated with the Rood phase of the Mississippian period has been excavated at the Singer Moye site (see Schnell et al. 1981). Ceramics of the Rood phase have grit and shell tempering, are mostly undecorated, and jars often have handles.

An important ceremonial center associated with this Mississippian phase in southwest Georgia is the Cemochechobee site, excavated from 1976-78. Believed to date from A.D. 900-1400, the site consists of the remains of a large village surrounding three temple mounds on the Chattahoochee River in Clay County. Excavations revealed numerous burials, structures and ceramic remains of major importance in the study of southwest Georgia prehistory during the Mississippian (see Schnell et al. *op. cit.*).

The Mississippian period on the Georgia coast is marked by ceramics identified as St. Catherines types. Although the late Woodland Wilmington cord-marked pottery continued to be made into early Mississippian times, increasing amounts of St. Catherines ceramic types are seen. Believed to date from A.D. 1000-1150, St. Catherines ceramics are tempered with clay and bear fine cord-marked impressions or net impressions. Some other vessels were either plain or had a burnished surface. The succeeding Savannah phase of the coastal Mississippian is sub-divided into at least two ceramic periods spanning the time A.D. 1150-1300. Savannah I ceramics, at least in the central coastal region, are marked by a decrease in cord-marked pottery and plain pottery, and an increase in check-stamped decoration. Savannah II ceramics show a return of cord-marked decoration, along with complicated stamped designs (Milanich 1977; DePratter and Howard 1980; Larsen 1982).

The final phase of the Mississippian on the Georgia coast is the Irene phase (1300-1550), named for the Irene site near Savannah. The Irene site was excavated 1937-40, and consisted of a temple mound and a burial mound. The temple mound exhibited eight phases of construction, and excavations here and in the burial mound made possible the establishment of a ceramic chronology for the northern Georgia coast. The ceramic style named Irene was the latest and persisted into the early historic period. It is typified by complicated stamped designs, incised decorations, and plain

Late Mississippian potsherd from the Georgia coast bearing complicated stamped designs. *(Liberty County; from a private collection)* Photo No. 58

or burnished vessels. The burial mound contained 106 burials, some of which contained pottery vessels and other objects.

Nearby, the remains of a structure, apparently a mortuary, were excavated. The building had been semi-subterranean, of wattle and daub construction, and was square with rounded corners. Fire had destroyed the building, accounting for the remarkable state of preservation of the remains, and the whole had been covered in sand. Each side of the building was approximately twenty-four feet long. Some wall post sections remained, allowing for their identification as yellow pine, and standing wall plaster remained, in some places up to fourteen inches high. The thickness of the interior plaster was about 1½ inches, and it contained impressions of the reeds and wall posts of the structure. The plaster also indicated that bundles of wild grape vines (?) had been interlaced at relatively short intervals between the upright posts. The plaster itself was of clay heavily tempered with a vegetal binder (possibly Spanish moss) (Caldwell and McCann 1941).

Finally, archaeologists discovered what they believed to be the remains of a council house at the Irene site. Situated near the large mound, it was a circular building with a diameter of approximately 120 feet. Caldwell and McCann (*op. cit.*) compare the remains uncovered there to descriptions of early Creek council houses and find that the descriptions vary somewhat, but in general are very useful in interpreting the supposed council house at Irene.

Irene ceramics were decorated by complicated stamping, incising, or burnishing, and all three decorative methods were sometimes employed on a single vessel. The Irene period in coastal Georgia prehistory persisted to the time of European contact.

The final phase of the Mississippian over much of Georgia is identified by Lamar pottery with all its local and regional variants. The original Lamar site is near Macon and was excavated in 1933-4. The ceramics at this site are described as exhibiting complicated stamped designs, but the wooden paddles used in applying the designs were poorly carved and the designs were applied to the vessel in a careless manner. The result was a confusion of blurred and overstamped designs (Kelly 1938:47). Some vessels display incised designs around the rim, but often these designs, too, are rather poorly executed.

The Lamar site consisted of a large temple mound, a smaller conical mound with a spiral ramp winding up its slopes, and a fairly small village area. In all, the site covered some twenty-one acres and was surrounded by a log palisade. This palisade was found to be 3,560 feet in length and contained posts six to twelve inches in diameter set about a foot apart (Fairbanks n.d.). Remains of what appear to be palisades have been noticed at some other sites of the Lamar phase in Georgia, and such palisades can be seen in the earliest paintings and engravings of Indian villages in the Southeast made by European explorers.

Numerous other Lamar sites have been excavated, and the results of these investigations have done much to expand our knowledge of this last Mississippian phase. Among those sites are: the Tugalo mound and village site, Stephens County (Caldwell 1974); the Nacoochee Mound, White County (Heye et al. 1918); the Rembert mounds, Elbert County (Caldwell 1953); the Bell Field Mound, Murray County (Kelly n.d.); and the Little Egypt mounds, Murray County (Hally 1979). The later Lamar ceramics overlap with historic-period artifacts over much of Georgia. Indeed, the Cherokees in northern Georgia were using Lamar ceramic styles well into historic times.

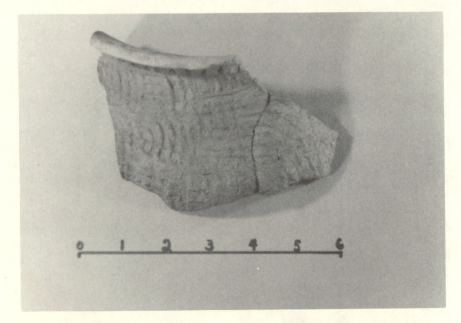

Lamar complicated stamped designs on a large potsherd. *(Banks County; from a private collection)* **Photo No. 59**

Lamar bold-incised decorations on a pot fragment. *(Banks County; from a private collection)* Photo No. 60

The spiral mound at the Lamar site after partial clearing. *(Courtesy National Park Service, Ocmulgee National Monument)* Photo No. 61

111

Summary

The distinguishing trait of the Mississippian period in Georgia is the agricultural economy of its people. Up until this time, agriculture had been of only minimal importance, but rather suddenly it became the economic base. At first, agricultural peoples seem to have established outposts, as at Ocmulgee, near Macon, which were surrounded by non-agricultural peoples. A ditch and/or log palisade surrounding the village, or at least the ceremonial area, came to be a feature at many if not most Mississippian sites. The larger sites are often centered about a temple mound or mound complex, which was associated with a religious or ceremonial system widespread in the Southeast at this time and which transcended tribal and linguistic differences. Eventually, all the native peoples of Georgia took up the agricultural way of life, although cultivated crops seem to have been of lesser importance to tribes in the coastal area.

The subsistence pattern of Mississippian peoples deserves a closer look, as it received only brief mention in the foregoing pages. Their agriculture was conducted without metal tools of any kind. Thus, the easily tilled soils in the riverbottoms were ideal, for they could be cleared relatively easily and were easily worked with the stone hoe and wooden digging stick. Stone or bone hoes and wooden digging sticks apparently were the only agricultural implements. Crops were maize, squash, beans, sunflower, and possibly some lesser known plants (such as lamb's quarters and amaranth) which have reverted to the wild state. Such produce was supplemented by hunting, gathering, and fishing activities. The bow and arrow was used in hunting, with the arrow being tipped with a small triangular stone point. Statewide, the white-tailed deer and the wild turkey were the most heavily exploited game, with bear, buffalo, and small game animals being important food items. Gathering activities centered primarily on procuring acorns, hickory nuts, walnuts, chestnuts (in northern Georgia), and various berries and fruits. Along the coast, various shellfish and marine or estuary foods were important.

While the ceremonialism of the "Southern Cult" was in a state of decline, and actually disappeared in some areas, other aspects of late Mississippian life carried over into the historic period. Thus, early descriptions of Indian life in Georgia left by traders, military expeditions, government agents, and travelers are invaluable not only for learning about Georgia's historic tribes, but also for interpreting what we find on late Mississippian sites. There follows an account of the tribes living in Georgia when the Europeans arrived.

REFERENCES: CHAPTER VI

Caldwell, Joseph R., and Catherine McCann, *Irene Mound Site, Chatham County, Georgia*, Uni-
1941   versity of Georgia Press, Athens.

_____, "A Preliminary Report on Excavations in the Allatoona Reservoir,"
1950   *Early Georgia*, Vol. 1, pp. 4-21.

———————————————, "The Rembert Mounds, Elbert County, Georgia," *Bureau of*
1953   *American Ethnology, Bulletin 154*, pp. 303-320.

———————————————, "Investigations at Rood's Landing, Stewart County, Georgia,"
1955   *Early Georgia*, Vol. 2, pp. 22-47.

———————————————, "Appraisal of the Archaeological Resources of Hartwell Reservoir,
1974   South Carolina and Georgia," *The Notebook, Institute of Archaeology and Anthropology,*
University of South Carolina, Columbia.

DePratter, Chester B., and James D. Howard, "Indian Occupation and Geologic History of the
1980   Georgia Coast: a 5,000 Year Summary," in *Excursions in Southeastern Geology: The
Archaeology-Geology of the Georgia Coast,* ed. by James D. Howard, Chester B. DePratter,
and Robert W. Frey, Guidebook 20, Georgia Geologic Survey, Department of Natural
Resources, Atlanta, pp. 1-65.

Fairbanks, Charles H., "The Lamar Palisade," Manuscript, Department of Anthropology, Univers-
n.d.   ity of Georgia, Athens.

———————————————, "The Macon Earth Lodge," *American Antiquity*, Vol. 2, pp. 94-
1946   108.

———————————————, *Archaeology of the Funeral Mound, Ocmulgee National Monu-
1956   ment, Georgia,* Archaeological Research Series, No. 3, U.S. Department of the Interior,
Washington.

Hally, David J., *Archaeological Investigation of the Little Egypt Site (9Mu102), Murray County,
1979   Georgia, 1969 Season,* University of Georgia, Laboratory of Archaeology Series, Report
No. 18, Athens.

Heye, George G., F.W. Hodge, and G.H. Pepper, *The Nacoochee Mound in Georgia,* Contributions
1918   from the Heye Museum of the American Indian, Vol. 2, No. 1.

Kelly, A.R., "A Preliminary Report on Archaeological Explorations at Macon, Georgia," *Bureau
1938   of American Ethnology, Bulletin 119,* pp. 1-69.

———————————————, "Explorations at Bell Field Mound and Village, Seasons 1965,
n.d.   1966, 1967, 1968," Unpublished Manuscript, Department of Anthropology, University of
Georgia, Athens.

———————————————, and Lewis H. Larson, Jr., "Explorations at Etowah Indian Mounds
1956   Near Cartersville, Georgia, Seasons 1954, 1955, 1956," *Archaeology,* Vol. 10, pp. 39-48.

Larsen, Clark Spencer, *The Anthropology of St. Catherines Island 3: Prehistoric Human Biolo-
1982   gical Adaptation,* Anthropological Papers of the American Museum of Natural History, Vol.
57, Part 3, New York.

Larson, Lewis H., Jr., "A Mississippian Headdress from Etowah, Georgia," *American Antiquity,*
1959   Vol. 25, No. 1, pp. 109-112.

———————————————, "Archaeological Implications of Social Stratification at the Etowah
1971   Site, Georgia," in *Approaches to the Social Dimensions of Mortuary Practices,* ed. by James
A. Brown, Memoirs of the Society for American Archaeology, No. 25.

Lee, Chung Ho, *The Beaverdam Creek Mound (9EB85), Elbert County, Georgia,* Department of
1976   Anthropology, University of Georgia, Athens.

Milanich, Jerald T., "A Chronology for the Aboriginal Cultures of Northern St. Simons Island,
1977   Georgia," *Florida Anthropologist,* Vol. 30, pp. 134-142.

Moorehead, Warren K., *Etowah Papers,* Department of Archaeology, Phillips Academy, Andover,
1979   Mass. (reprint of the 1932 edition by Charley G. Drake, Union City, Georgia).

Rudolph, James L., and David J. Hally, "Archaeological Investigation of the Beaverdam Creek
1984   Site (9ED85), Elbert County, Georgia," Draft Report Submitted to the Atlanta Archaeological Services Branch of the National Park Service.

Schnell, Frank T., Vernon J. Knight, Jr., and Gail S. Schnell, *Cemochechobee: Archaeology of a
1981   Mississippian Ceremonial Center on the Chattahoochee River,* University Presses of Florida,
Gainesville.

Taylor, Richard L., and Marion F. Smith, *The Report of the Intensive Survey of the Richard B.*
1978 *Russell Dam and Lake, Savannah River, Georgia and South Carolina,* Research Manuscript
Series 142, Institute of Archaeology and Anthropology, University of South Carolina,
Columbia, South Carolina.

Wauchope, Robert, *Archaeological Survey of Northern Georgia,* Memoirs of the Society for
1966 American Archaeology, No. 21, Salt Lake City.

Wilson, Rex L., "A Radiocarbon Date for the Macon Earth Lodge," *American Antiquity,* Vol. 30,
1964 pp. 202.

Chapter VII

GEORGIA'S HISTORIC TRIBES

*T*he Indian peoples living in what is now Georgia during the historic period were found to have been practicing an economy based on agriculture, hunting, fishing, and gathering. In some cases, they are believed to have been the direct descendants of some of the prehistoric cultures discussed in the foregoing pages. In other cases, some groups are known to have only recently moved into the area. However, they shared many things in common. Their hunting and gathering practices can be traced back to the Archaic. Despite similarities in some areas, Georgia's historic tribes were quite diverse in others. There follows a brief overview of the Indian peoples of Georgia known to early explorers, traders, and settlers. Their names for many of Georgia's creeks, rivers, and mountains are still used, and although they are gone, their memory and their mark on the land and on Georgia's history remains.

THE CREEKS

Most of the area of what is now Georgia was occupied by Indians belonging to the Creek Confederacy in early historic times. The name "Creek" originated from a shortening of Ocheese Creek Indians, the name given by the English to the native peoples living along Ocheese Creek (Ocmulgee River). In time, the name came to be applied to all those groups in the Creek Confederacy. The dominant group in this alliance called themselves Muskogee in later times, although this word has no meaning in their language and is of uncertain origin. The Muskogee group was composed of twelve bands: Kasihta, Coweta, Coosa, Abihka, Wakokai, Eufaula, Hilibi, Atasi, Kolomi, Tukabahchee, Pakana, and Okchai (Swanton 1922:215). In time, these came to be known as the Upper Creeks (those living along the Coosa, Tallapoosa, and Alabama Rivers) and the Lower Creeks (those living along the Flint and lower Chattahoochee Rivers). These tribes all spoke languages belonging to the Muskogean linguistic family, a widespread language group in the Southeast that includes the languages of the Choctaw and Chickasaw. Other tribes related to the Creeks in Georgia included: the Guale (living along the coast from near Savannah to St. Andrews Sound), Apalachee (probably occupied a small portion of southwest Georgia), Apalachicola (originally living in southwest Georgia, they moved to the Savannah River, then to the Chattahoochee River), Chiaha (in Colonial times, this group was living among the Lower Creeks on the

Chattahoochee River), Hitchiti (probably once occupied most of southern Georgia), Okmulgee (probably a branch of the Hitchiti living in what is now Butts County), Oconee (lived on the Oconee River in the vicinity of what is now Milledgeville), and Tamahita (lived on the Chattahoochee River among the Lower Creeks in early Colonial times) (for further information see Swanton 1922).

Creek towns or settlements were located along the rivers of their territory. Consisting of from thirty to a hundred or more houses, these settlements were strung out along the rivers, with a more or less concentration of houses near the ceremonial area. In border areas, however, villages were more compact and were fortified. Bartram (1955:168-9) describes the habitations of the Alachua (Oconee) as having:

". . . . two houses nearly the same size about thirty feet in length, twelve feet wide, and about the same in height. The door is placed midway on one side or in the front. This house is divided equally, across, into two apartments, one of which is the cook room. The other house is nearly of the same dimensions, standing about twenty yards from the dwelling house, its end fronting the door. The building is two stories high and constructed in a different manner. It is divided transversely, as the other, but the end next the dwelling house is open on three sides, supported by posts or pillars. It has an open loft or platform, the ascent to which is by a portable stair or ladder: this is a pleasant, cool, airy situation, and here the master or chief of the family retires to repose in the hot seasons, and receives his guests or visitors. The other half of this building is closed on all sides by notched logs; the lowest or ground part is a potatoe house, and the upper story over it is a granary for corn and other provisions. Their houses are constructed of a kind of frame. In the first place, strong corner pillars are fixed in the ground, with others somewhat less, ranging on a line between; these are strengthened by cross pieces of timber, and the whole with the roof is covered close with the bark of the Cypress tree."

(from Bartram 1955:168)

However, Bartram found another type of arrangement at a Muskogee town on the Tallapoosa River. He writes:

". . . . every habitation consists of four oblong square houses, of one story, of the same form and dimensions, and so situated as to form an exact square, encompassing an area or court yard of about a quarter of an acre of ground. . ."

(Bartram *op. cit.*:318)

Of the Creeks themselves, Bartram described the women as ". . . remarkably short of stature" but well-proportioned, "their visage round, features regular and beautiful . . . . the eye large, black, and languishing, expressive of modesty, diffidence, and bashfulness . . ." The Creek men were tall, many above six feet, and their complexion was darker than that of the other tribes visited by Bartram (*op. cit.*:380-81). Gen. Oglethorpe said the Indians living near the newly established settlement of Savannah anointed themselves with oil and exposed themselves to the sun. He described the men as being decorated with red, blue, yellow, and black paints and wearing a breech-

Yoholo-Micco, a Creek leader during the early 1800's. *(Courtesy Hargrett Rare Book and Manuscript Library, University of Georgia Libraries)* **Photo No. 62**

Opothle-yoholo, an outspoken opponent of the Creek removal treaty. *(Courtesy Hargrett Rare Book and Manuscript Library, University of Georgia Libraries)* **Photo No. 63**

clout. The women wore a skirt which reached to the knees. In winter, both men and women wrapped a mantle about them, leaving the arms bare (in Jones 1873:86).

Somewhat later, Bartram recorded that Creek men shaved their head, leaving only a narrow crest of hair beginning at the top of the head, gradually widening towards the back. Thus, the back of the head and neck was left covered in hair, which was allowed to grow long and was decorated with pendants and quills. They also wore a band about four inches wide about their head. This band was decorated with stones, beads, and other items, and a peak in the front was embellished with a long plume of crane or heron feathers (Bartram *op. cit.*:393). Clothing consisted of a linen shirt, breechclout, cloth leggings, and moccasins.

Creek women wore a short waistcoat and a skirt which reached to the middle of the leg. Their hair was worn plaited and fastened at the crown of the head with a silver brooch. On festive occasions, a large quantity of ribbons of many colors decorated their hair, streaming down on every side almost to the ground.

Bartram described the Creeks in general as having the bearing of a great hero:

"A proud, haughty and arrogant race of men; they are brave and valiant in war, ambitious of conquest, restless and perpetually exercising their arms, yet magnanimous and merciful to a vanquished enemy, when he submits and seeks their friendship and protection."

(Bartram *op. cit.*:382-3)

Creek women have played important roles in the political and social life of members of this confederacy throughout the historic period. As early as 1540, there were female political leaders, for the De Soto expedition records the following:

". . . . the Cacica came out of the town, seated in a chair, which some principal men having borne to the bank, she entered a canoe. Over the stern was an awning, and in the bottom lay extended a mat where were two cushions, one above the other, upon which she sate; and she was accompanied by her chief men . . . "

(Bourne 1973:65)

Women also owned the houses and were permanent occupants, while aged men whose wives had died generally went to live in households belonging to the women of their own clan. As was generally the case among the southeastern tribes, clan membership was matrilineal, i.e., one belonged to one's mother's clan (see Hudson 1976). Bartram records that Creek women were held in high regard by the men and that he never knew of an instance of abuse, although other writers noted that Creek women were required to do the heavy work of harvesting and cutting wood for the winter (see Swanton 1928a:387).

Creek government was based in the talwa, or town, which consisted of a ceremonial and political center with all its outlying villages and settlements. Like other tribes in the Southeast, the Creeks had a Red (war) and White (peace) dichotomy which included clans and towns. A White talwa, or town, was presided over by a miko, or White chief. Bartram says the following regarding the White chief among the Creeks:

"He has the disposal of the corn and fruits, and gives audience to ambassadors, deputies, and strangers who come to the town or tribe, receives presents, etc. . . ."

(in Swanton 1928a:278)

This White chief was the head of the tribal council and was its spokesman. He was assisted by a vice-chief and a body of lesser chiefs representing various clans (see Swanton *op. cit.*). Red towns, on the other hand, were associated with war. Concerning the Red chief, Milfort says the following:

"His mission consisted in directing all of the war operations, in taking all measures necessary to revenge an injury inflicted on the nation and in defending its rights. He was invested with authority sufficient for this purpose . . . once peace was reestablished and the troops returned . . . he again became a plain citizen . . ."

(in Swanton 1928a:298)

So, while some towns were traditionally known as White towns and others as Red towns, each town had a White chief, and theoretically each town would contain warriors from among whom a War leader would be chosen.

Creek ceremonialism played a vital role in tribal life. The Creek New Year began with the appearance of a new moon in midsummer (July or August) and was marked by the Busk (Boskita) ceremony. After a day of feasting, the Busk ceremony began with a dance by the women of the town. This dance was followed by a ball game played by the young men. Afterwards, the chief prepared the sacred medicines to be used the next day, when the New Fire Ceremony was performed. In this part of the Busk, four logs were cut and brought to the squareground. All fires in the town were extinguished and pots used in cooking over the old fires were broken. The fire-maker, dressed in white, then approached the fireplace in the square and ceremoniously kindled a new fire. The four logs were pushed into this new fire, and the first ears of corn from the new crop were placed on the fire as offerings. Coals from this fire were then used to re-kindle household fires throughout the town. Herbal medicines were then served to everyone in order to purify the body and soul.

Sometime after this phase of the ceremony, the famous "Black Drink" was taken. Brewed from several different kinds of leaves and herbs, it was an emetic and thus was immediately vomited up. It was believed to purify the body and mind of those who took it. The importance of the Black Drink in Creek social and religious life is indicated by the following statement:

". . . . they have a religious belief that it infallibly possesses the following qualities, viz.: That it purifies them from all sin, and leaves them with an invincible prowess in war; and that it is the only solid cement of friendship, benevolence, and hospitality."

(in Swanton 1928b:538)

After more dancing and speech-making, the Busk ended.

120

Swanton records that purely social dances were popular and were generally held when the moon was full. Ceremonies, on the other hand, usually took place at the time of the new moon (Swanton 1928b:522).

As was the case with many other southeastern tribes, the Creeks were exposed to Christian teachings in early historic times (see Hudson *op. cit.*). The result has been that original religious beliefs have been obscured, forgotten, or highly colored by Christianity. In writing on this subject, Swanton found that in historic times, the Creeks referred to the supreme diety as the Master of Breath or the Breath Holder (1928b:481). He further notes that an earlier belief in the One Above is evident, and that this being was associated with fire. Swanton writes:

"All of the facts brought out must mean that an actual connection was supposed to exist between the sun and the busk fire and thus between the celestial diety behind the sun and this fire, and . . . that the renewal of this fire was an actual renewed presence of the diety among them . . ."

(Swanton 1928b:484)

In addition to the Breath Holder, the Creeks believed in many other spirit beings.

An important element in Creek society was the clan system. The Creeks had more than fifty clans (Bear, Fox, Raccoon, Alligator, Cane, Red Paint, et al.), all of which were matrilineal, i.e., one belonged to one's mother's clan. Several clans would be represented in any given Creek town, and all members of the clan were considered as being related. Thus, a visitor to a town would be provided with food and lodging by a member of his or her clan. It has been suggested that the clan system formed one of the strongest unifying forces among the various bands, tribes, and groups of the Creek Confederacy (Spencer and Jennings 1977:435).

Some clans were considered to be related, and thus formed larger groupings called phratries. Such groupings tended to be seated together in the squareground during the Busk ceremony (*op. cit.*:436).

The Creek economy consisted of a combination of agriculture, hunting, fishing, and gathering. Agriculture was perhaps the most important, and Adair recorded that Creek men helped the women "plant a sufficient plenty of provisions" before they left on summertime war expeditions (in Williams 1930:276). Bartram observed that at the Seminole town of Aluchua in northern Florida, small garden plots containing beans, tobacco, some corn and other fruits and vegetables were planted near each dwelling, but the main fields of corn, squash, pumpkin, and other vegetables were located some distance away (Bartram 1955:169). He indicates that these larger fields were planted cooperatively and a portion of the harvest was deposited in a public granary. This was in turn to be used by the needy, to be given to other towns in case their crops were destroyed, to supply war parties, and any other needs (*op. cit.*:401). Stone or bone hoes along with digging sticks were the chief agricultural implements prior to the acquisition of European tools.

In addition to agriculture, many wild plants, fruits, nuts, and berries were gathered. As most other southeastern tribes, they readily adopted cultivated plants introduced by the Europeans. A description of the Creek fare is contained in Romans (as quoted in Swanton 1946:285):

"... they dry peaches and persimmons, chestnuts and the fruit of the *Cham-aerops* [*Rhapidophyllum hystrix*], the "needle palm," they also prepare a cake of the pulp of the species of the *passi flora,* vulgarly called may apple; some kinds of acorns they also prepare into good bread. . . ."

In this passage, Romans mistakenly refers to the edible maypop (*Passiflora incarnata*) as a mayapple. Bartram (in Swanton *op. cit.*:287) adds:

"But, besides the cultivated fruits . . . they have in use a vast variety of wild or native vegetables, both fruits and roots . . ."

Bartram goes on to list the products of various plants then in use among the Creeks, including persimmons, mulberries, honey locust, hickory nuts, acorns, grapes, and smilax roots (*Smilax pseudochina*). Many of these items, along with agricultural products, were preserved for use in winter by drying them in the sun.

Members of the Creek Confederacy set out in search of game in autumn, traveling as family units. One writer mentions that these families only returned to the towns in March, laden with skins and smoked meat (in Swanton 1946:263). Hawkins (1916: 385-6) also mentions that the Creeks went on an extended hunt, returning to the towns in late February or March. Deer was the primary quarry, but bear oil was widely used in cooking and thus this species was a prime target as well. While the larger game was taken by means of a bow and arrow, smaller animals and birds were killed by means of a blowgun. Romans (in Swanton 1946:285) notes that the Creek diet included deer, bear, turkey, and smaller game, all of which "they spare not." He also writes that they enjoyed freshwater turtle and "plenty of fish."

One method of procuring fish which was widely used by the Creeks and other tribes is described by Adair as follows:

"In a dry summer season, they gather horse chestnuts, and different sorts of roots, which having pounded pretty fine, and steeped a while in a trough, they scatter this mixture over the surface of a middle-sized pond, and stir it about with poles, till the water is sufficiently impregnated with the intoxicating bittern. The fish are soon inebriated, and make to the surface of the water, with their bellies uppermost. The fishers gather them in baskets . . . fish catched in this manner are not poisoned, but only stupefied; for they prove very wholesome food . . ."

(in Williams 1930:432)

Fish were also taken in traps, by hook and line, by spearing, and by shooting them with arrows.

This pattern of hunting, gathering, fishing, and agriculture served the Creeks and surrounding peoples well. If a crop failed, they still had many resources to fall back on which would provide sustenance until another crop could be raised. This pattern was disrupted by the Europeans, however, for not only did subsistence patterns change as a result of introduced crops and techniques, not to mention the demands of the fur trade, but pressure for land meant the abandonment of former hunting and gathering territory.

The Creeks were first contacted by the De Soto expedition of 1540, and intermittent contacts with the Spanish continued as exploratory expeditions crossed Creek territory and missions were established along the coast. With the beginning of the fur trade, propagated by the English, the Creek lifeway began to change drastically. Deer were hunted primarily or solely for their skins and tens of thousands of hides were traded to the English (see Crane 1928:111). Some Lower Creeks moved eastward so as to be nearer the traders, but dishonest traders caused discontent among the Indians. This culminated in the Yamassee War in 1715, in which the Creeks played a part. The English soundly defeated the Indians, however, and the Creeks began withdrawing westward. The Lower Creeks moved their towns from the Ocmulgee River westward to the lower Chattahoochee.

Because of their long-standing ties to the British, the Creeks supported them during the American Revolution. After the Revolution, some Creeks accepted programs of aid from the new government of the United States and prospered, some becoming substantial farmers and slave-owners. However, other Creeks tried to maintain a more traditional lifestyle, and it was this faction which again joined the British during the War of 1812. Following defeat again, the Creeks in general were forced into land cessions. Some whites continued to agitate for the cession of all Creek lands, and a Creek leader, William McIntosh, signed a document in 1825 which ceded all Creek lands east of the Mississippi in return for land in what would later become Oklahoma. He lacked any authority to sign such an agreement and he was murdered for doing so, but the U.S. government chose to regard the treaty as legitimate and in 1835-40, forced the Creeks and their allies to move West (see Spencer and Jennings 1977:425; et al.). Creek lands in Georgia and other states were quickly occupied by whites and the sites of former Indian settlements were plowed and put into cultivation by their new owners.

THE CHEROKEES

Much of the northern portion of Georgia was the home of the Cherokees during the early historic period. According to traditions of both Creeks and Cherokees, the Creeks were the original possessors of the land, but the Cherokees had begun to displace them prior to white contact. This Cherokee expansion continued well into the Colonial period and ultimately they occupied all of north Georgia. Cherokee legends indicate that they moved south into the Southern Appalachians from somewhere to the north, possibly the upper Ohio drainage. This legend is given credence by linguistic, cultural, and archaeological evidence.

The name "Cherokee" is of uncertain origin and has no meaning in the native language of this tribe. They referred to themselves as Yun-wiya, meaning "real people" or "principle people" (Mooney 1900:15). Both linguistically and culturally, they are related to the Iroquois tribes of the northeastern United States, and it is generally believed that they broke away from the main body several centuries ago and moved southward, ultimately settling in the Southern Appalachians. It was here that they were first contacted by Europeans. The Cherokees were found to be living in permanent villages or towns situated in the broad riverbottoms along the major streams in their territory. Such towns varied in size, the largest containing populations of five hundred or more (Gearing 1962:1). These settlements were for the most part composed of individual houses located in random fashion up and down the riverbottoms for a mile or more, with a heavier concentration of houses near the council house and the chief's residence. The botanist, William Bartram, described such a Cherokee town in 1776 in the following terms:

> "Riding through this large town [Whatoga], the road carried me winding about through their little plantations of Corn, Beans, etc. up to the council-house ... All before me and on every side, appeared little plantations of young Corn, Beans, etc. divided from each other by narrow strips or borders of grass, which marked the bounds of each one's property, their habitation standing in the midst."
>
> (Bartram 1955:284)

Bartram further describes 18th century Cherokee houses in the following manner:

> "The Cherokees construct their habitations on a different plan from the Creeks; that is, but one oblong four square building, of one story high; the materials consisting of logs or trunks of trees, stripped of their bark, notched at their ends, fixed one upon another, and afterwards plaistered well, both inside and out, with clay tempered with dry grass, and the whole covered or roofed with the bark of the chestnut tree or long broad shingles."
>
> (Bartram op. cit.:296)

While this dispersed manner seems to have been the preferred settlement pattern of the Cherokees, those towns located near border areas were often more compact and rather heavily fortified (see Malone 1956:13-14).

Lieut. Henry Timberlake, an English officer who spent some time among the Cherokees in the 1760's, described them as being "of a middle stature, of an olive color," though heavily painted and tattooed (in Williams 1948:75). Bartram (op. cit.: 381) said they were taller and more robust than the Creeks, and he found Cherokee women "tall, erect—and of a delicate frame" (p. 380). Timberlake (ibid.) also records that Cherokee men shaved their head or plucked their hair, leaving only a scalplock on the back of the head. This they decorated with "beads, feathers, wampum, stained deer's hair, and such like baubles." Women wore their hair long and decorated it with ribbons." Already the Cherokees had largely adopted European clothing, but old people informed Timberlake that formerly they wore little clothing, "except a bit of skin about their middles, mockasons, a mantle of buffalo skin for the winter, and a lighter one of feathers for the summer" (op. cit.:77).

In general, Bartram found the Cherokee disposition and manner grave and steady, and described them as being "dignified and circumspect in their deportment; rather slow and reserved in conversation; yet frank, cheerful, and humane." (op. cit.:381). Timberlake said they had a gentle and amicable disposition, towards their friends, but could be implacable enemies. He also remarked that they were very hardy, "bearing heat, cold, hunger and thirst, in a surprizing manner" (p. 78). Furthermore, "they are extremely proud, despising the lower class of Europeans" (p. 79).

Too-an-Tuh, or Spring Frog, a Cherokee of the early 1800's. *(Courtesy Hargrett Rare Book and Manuscript Library, University of Georgia Libraries)* **Photo No. 64**

Tahchee, or Dutch, a Cherokee scout. *(Courtesy Hargrett Rare Book and Manuscript Library, University of Georgia Libraries)* **Photo No. 65**

Women occupied a prominent and important place in Cherokee society. Certain women, called "war-women" in the early historic literature, participated in tribal councils and indeed, they decided whether prisoners were to be tortured to death or adopted into the tribe. A woman occupying this office was also called "Beloved Woman," "Pretty Woman," and "Honored Woman." Some idea of the powerful position occupied by these matrons can be gained from the historic record, for the "War Woman of Chota" addressed the Hopewell treaty conference in 1785. Their participation in the "manly" arts went beyond government, however, for Timberlake records that "many of the Indian women [are] as famous in war, as powerful in the council" (in Williams op. cit.:93).

Cherokee tribal government consisted of a Red organization and a White organization, which were roughly equivalent to what we know as martial law and civil law. In addition to functions of government, officials also had numerous ceremonial or religious duties to perform which were often interconnected with the operation of government. Each of the two divisions had its own officials and its own functions to perform. During times of peace, the White organization operated the affairs of the tribe. The office of White chief, or uku, was the highest political office in the tribe, and although each town had its own White chief, the White chief of the capital town was regarded as chief of the nation. This office appears to have been mostly hereditary, passing from the chief to his oldest sister's son. Also, the wife of the White chief was regarded as a very important person and if the White chief died suddenly she could assume his office until a substitute was appointed (Gilbert 1943:321).

Certain towns were known as White towns and were regarded as places of refuge. The White organization was all-powerful in these towns and could grant reprieve even to those seeking to escape blood revenge. Non-political functions of White organization officials are summed up by Gilbert as follows:

"They alone possessed prayers for invoking the sun and moon and other protective spirits who could take away disease and ill health. They could separate the unclean elements from polluted persons and restore the normal condition. Their persons and belongings were sacred and were not like ordinary citizens and their possessions. The sacredness of the white officials was so great as to separate them as a class superior to the rest of the community and in some respects above the ordinary laws and usages."

(Gilbert 1943:357)

The Red organization came to power when the tribe was at war. The warriors elected a Great War Captain subject to the approval of the White chief, and in addition, each town had a war chief. Ceremonial functions of the Red organization included the ritual purification of warriors both before and after hostilities, as blood was considered spiritually contaminating (see Gilbert ibid.). Forms of divination were employed in order to attempt to forecast the outcome of a war expedition, and every magical precaution was taken by participants in a raid to ensure personal well-being.

Tribal life among the Cherokees was marked by the alternation of war and peace, and also by the observance of several important ceremonies. These ceremonies were designed to ensure the physical and spiritual well-being of the tribe and were scheduled to correspond to particular lunar phases or stages in the crop season. The Cherokee new year began with the new moon in October, autumn being the season during which they believed the world had been created. This was also the time for observing the Great New Moon Ceremony, which consisted of feasting, dancing, and religious observances. Near the end of October, the most significant religious ceremony of the year was held—the Reconciliation, or "Friends Made" Ceremony. During this ceremony, vows of perpetual friendship were made and reconciliation between parties in a dispute was effected. Furthermore, this ceremony symbolized the uniting of the people with the Supreme Being, and it was believed to purify their minds and bodies (Lewis and Kneberg 1958:183).

Sometime in December, the Exalting, or Bounding Bush Ceremony was held. Little is known about this observance, except that it appears to have been largely secular and involved dances which ended at midnight for three consecutive nights. On the fourth night, there was a feast before the dancing began and tobacco and pine needles were thrown by the dancers into the fire. Lewis and Kneberg (*op. cit.*:185) interpret this act as a symbolic sacrifice.

When the grass began to grow and trees began to put on new leaves, the Cherokees observed the first new moon of spring. A central part of this ceremony involved predicting the success or failure of the crops by the chief, who gazed into a sacred quartz crystal to receive his prognostication. Seven days after this rite, the people extinguished the fire in the temple and kindled a new fire, using wood from seven different species of trees. In time, everyone was given embers or coals from this sacred fire to carry home and thus light new fires throughout the land.

In late summer when the corn became ripe enough to eat, the Green Corn Ceremony was held. Common among the southeastern tribes, this ceremony was a thanksgiving rite and involved offerings of new corn and a deer's tongue. The Cherokees used seven ears of corn, each ear coming from the field of a different clan. After this had been offered, and other rituals had been observed, a feast prepared from the new corn was enjoyed by the people.

Still another of the yearly ceremonies observed by the Cherokee had to do with the corn crop. This was the Ripe Corn Ceremony, which was primarily a harvest festival. It took place in late September and lasted four days (see Gilbert *op. cit.* and Kneberg *op. cit.* for more detail on the above ceremonies).

Every seventh year, a major thanksgiving ceremony replaced the Great New Moon Ceremony. This was the Uku dance and was the time when the uku, the White chief, was reconsecrated in his office of high priest. Amidst elaborate preparations and ritual, the White chief was divested of his usual white clothes and headdress, bathed, and dressed in new clothes and a new headdress, all dyed bright yellow. Dances and other solemn rituals were held, and on the fourth day, the uku was reinvested with his religious and civil powers by a prominent official.

In addition to these major ceremonies, Gilbert points out that minor local ceremonies were observed "at each quarter of the year, at each new moon, every seven days, and on each occasion of calamity or epidemic" (Gilbert, p. 326).

Since the Cherokees were heavily influenced by Christianity over an extended period of time, these ceremonies ceased to be performed at an early date. Likewise, because of Christian influence, little is now known of their ancient religion. Although there is some disagreement among authorities, it seems that the ancient Cherokees believed in one Supreme Being, whom they called Yowa. This Being was conceived of as a unity of three beings, referred to as "The Elder Fires Above." These were believed to have created the sun and moon and gave the world its form, but then had removed themselves to the seventh heaven. The sun and moon were left to finish the creation of the stars and all living things. Fire was appointed to be the protector of human beings and to be the intermediary between man and the sun. Smoke was the messenger, bearing man's prayers toward heaven (Lewis and Kneberg op. cit.:175-6). Thus the importance of sacrifices via the sacred fire in the temple and ritual smoking in council meetings is apparent.

Virtually every aspect of Cherokee life was influenced by the clan system. There were seven clans: Deer, Bird, Paint, Wolf, Blue (?), Wild Potato (?), and Twisters (?) [the English translation of the last three names remains uncertain]. Membership in each clan was matrilineal, i.e., one belonged to one's mother's clan. Each generation in a clan considered themselves to be brothers and sisters, and marriage to a member of one's own clan was thus considered incestuous and was strictly forbidden. The clan system served as a kind of uniting mechanism, for each clan was represented in every Cherokee settlement. A member of the tribe traveling to some other village would announce his clan upon entering the settlement. Immediately, he would be given food and lodging by some member of his clan who resided there. As is evident in the foregoing discussion on government and religion, the clans also had ceremonial and governmental functions.

The Cherokees, in keeping with all other tribes of the Southeast, had an economy based on agriculture, hunting, fishing, and gathering. Of these, agriculture perhaps was the most important, and their original crops consisted of corn (maize), beans, and squash (including pumpkins). Agricultural activities began in spring when fields were burned off and the ground was prepared for planting. The only agricultural implements were the digging stick and a stone or bone hoe. While the men helped in the heavy work of clearing land, preparing the ground for planting, and harvesting the crops, the rest of the agricultural work was left to the women. Timberlake observed that "Women alone do all the laborious tasks of agriculture, the soil requiring only a little stirring with a hoe, to produce whatever is required of it" (in Williams 1948:68).

According to Adair, an English trader from Charleston, the Cherokees spaced their corn hills about two feet apart in straight rows about a yard apart. Five or six grains of corn were planted in each hill, and pumpkins, sunflowers, and beans were planted in between (in Williams 1930:439). While small garden plots were found near individual dwellings, larger fields were located some distance away from the village (Williams op. cit.:438). The Cherokees readily accepted crops introduced by the Europeans and by the mid-eighteenth century, they were already growing peas, watermelons, and muskmelons as well as planting orchards of European fruit trees (Williams 1930:439; Corkran 1969:14).

Most of the agricultural products were preserved by drying them in the sun. Adair records that roasting-ears were boiled in the shuck, then dried. They were later boiled with venison and eaten. Green beans were dried and were a favorite winter food (these were also enjoyed by early white settlers, who called them "leather-britches"). The

Cherokees also dried the introduced foods, such as cabbage, apples, and peaches for winter fare.

Hunting was an important part of the economy of all the tribes of the Southeast, and the Cherokee country was particularly rich in game. Bartram (1976:31) indicates that most Cherokee hunting took place in the fall and winter months. Since game in the immediate vicinity of a settlement was soon depleted, it was necessary for hunters to travel some distance. Concerning the southeastern tribes in general, Adair observed:

> "Their manner of rambling through the woods to kill deer, is a very laborious exercise, as they frequently walk twenty-five or thirty miles through rough and smooth grounds, fasting, before they return to camp, loaded."
>
> (Williams 1930:432)

As is indicated, the deer was the primary quarry of Cherokee hunters, but bears were also sought, for bear grease was widely used in cooking. Buffalo and elk were present in early historic times and probably provided occasional meals. All larger game was killed with the bow and arrow, but smaller game (squirrels, rabbits, birds) were taken in traps of various kinds or were killed by means of the blowgun. The Cherokees made their bows from sycamore, hickory, or yellow locust wood (Lewis and Kneberg) 1958:77), and after shaping, the bow was soaked in bear grease and seasoned before the fire. The bow string was made of twisted bear gut or the twisted fibers of Indian hemp (*Apocynum cannabinum*). Arrow shafts were made from a species of cane (Lewis and Kneberg *ibid.*) or a sourwood shoot, and were tipped with triangular stone points, garfish scales, deer antler tips, or wild turkey spurs, and some shafts were simply sharpened and fire-hardened.

Timberlake recorded the following concerning Cherokee cooking:

> "After smoking, the eatables were produced, consisting chiefly of wild meat; such as vinison, bear, and buffalo; tho' I cannot much commend their cookery, everything being greatly overdone . . ."
>
> (Timberlake in Williams 1948:61)

He further records that "potatoes, pumpkins, hominy, boiled corn, beans, and pease" were served in small, flat baskets made of split cane (*ibid.*)

Fish was an important element in the Cherokee diet, and most fishing activity occurred during the warmer months. One popular method of catching fish is described by Adair as follows:

> "The Indians have the art of catching fish in long crails, made with canes and hickory splinters, tapering to a point. They lay these at a fall of water, where stones are placed in two sloping lines from each bank, till they meet together in the middle of the rapid stream, where the intangled fish are soon drowned. Above such a place, I have known them to fasten a wreath of long grape vines together, to reach across the river, with stones fastened at proper distances to rake the bottom; they will swim a mile with it whooping, and plunging all the way, driving the fish before them into their large cane pots. With this draught, which is a very heavy one, they make a town feast . . ."
>
> (Adair in Williams 1930:432-3)

Remains of the stone walls associated with this type of fish trap can still be seen in rivers throughout the former Cherokee country at times of low water. The Cherokees also procured fish by several other means (see White 1980).

The gathering of edible nuts, fruits, berries, and green plants was an important subsistence activity among the Cherokees. Some foods obtained by gathering, such as chestnuts and hickory nuts, were dietary staples, but most other foods procured in this manner were only seasonal additions to the diet. Some foods in the latter category are acorns, chinkapins, walnuts, "jellico" (*Ligusticum canadense*), "sochan" (*Rudbeckia laciniata*), blackberries, huckleberries, and wild strawberries. While nuts could be stored for extended periods of time, berries and greens were most often consumed soon after they were gathered, but some were dried to be eaten during the winter months.

As inferred from the foregoing brief account of Cherokee subsistence activities, theirs was a particularly rich environment. The mountains and foothills contained nut-bearing trees of several species, and birds and mammals thrived in such a situation. The rivers and creeks abounded in fish, and the riverbottoms contained rich, easily worked soil. All was not harmony, however, for intertribal wars and raids were ubiquitous, even before the Europeans appeared on the scene. With the coming of the white traders, explorers, and settlers, tribal life was drastically altered.

It appears that the Cherokees were never unified politically, certainly not during the early historic period. Their capital changed from town to town, depending upon the residence of the current principal chief. In 1715, the capital was at the town of Tugalo, on the Tugalo River in what is now Stephens County, Georgia, and Oconee County, South Carolina. By 1730, it was at Chota, on the Little Tennessee River in east Tennessee. A few years later, the capital was located in yet another town, and by the early 1800's, it was again in Georgia, this time at New Echota near the present Calhoun, Georgia.

Such political instability was undoubtedly exacerbated by the pressures of the time and by the Colonial powers, who encouraged Indian groups to war with one another, thus further decimating the native population. The Cherokees were gradually pushed out of northeast Georgia by the advancing tide of settlers, and expanded westward and southwestward at the expense of the Creeks. Resoundingly beaten by the American forces during the American Revolution (the Cherokees sided with the British), in the post-war years they accepted livestock, farming implements, etc. provided by the government as part of treaty obligations. They also accepted the teachings of missionaries and embarked on a new course, one patterned after the newly formed United States. However, despite all their accomplishments, forces in the United States government, both at the state and national levels, were urging that all Indians be removed to west of the Mississippi. After years of debate and court battles, the Treaty of Removal was signed by a few non-representative Cherokees in 1835, by which the tribe released claim on all its land in the East in return for land in Indian Territory (Oklahoma). Congress ratified the treaty, despite bitter debate, and when it became obvious that the Cherokees were not going to leave voluntarily, the Army was ordered to begin forcibly removing them. During 1838-39, the Cherokees were rounded up and placed in stockades for weeks, then were accompanied by the Army on the march to Indian Territory. Known as the infamous Trail of Tears, it was a trail of death and

John Ridge, a highly acculturated Cherokee of the early 1800's. *(Courtesy Hargrett Rare Book and Manuscript Library, University of Georgia Libraries)* **Photo No. 66**

suffering where some 4,000 Cherokees died of exposure and illness, for the march took place during a particularly harsh winter.

Today, rivers, towns, streets, parks, and historic sites commemorate the Cherokees in Georgia. Some residents of north Georgia can claim descent from Cherokees who married whites, for intermarriages were common in spite of the times. Those descendants of Indians in Georgia, be they Cherokee, Creek, or others, can be proud, for their ancestors lived here long before Oglethorpe sailed up the Savannah.

THE YUCHI

A tribal group which was widely known in Georgia in the early historic period was the Yuchi. Calling themselves Tsoyaha, "Offspring of the Sun," they lived in or near the Southern Appalachians, but during the seventeenth and early eighteenth centuries, most of them moved south into the low country, settling in several different locations (Swanton 1922:287, 289). Accordingly, one group settled on the Savannah River above what is now Augusta, but in later times moved to the Chattahoochee River. Another group settled on the lower Savannah River and later joined the Lower Creeks (*ibid.*). Bartram describes the Yuchi town on the Chattahoochee as follows:

"The Uche town is situated in a vast plain, on the plain, on the gradual ascent as we rise from a narrow strip of low ground immediately bordering on the river: it is the largest, most compact, and best situated Indian town I ever saw; the habitations are large and neatly built; the walls of the houses are constructed of a wooden frame, then lathed and plaistered inside and out with a reddish well tempered clay or mortar . . . and these houses are neatly covered or roofed with Cypress bark or shingles of that tree."

(Bartram 1955:312)

Apparently, no records exist of the physical appearance of the Yuchi in early historic times. All descriptions of them belong to the time when European trade goods had been adopted. These descriptions indicate that Yuchi men wore a brightly colored calico shirt, over which was worn a sleeved jacket reaching to the knee on old men and chiefs. Young men wore a shorter jacket. The long jacket was bound around the waist by a belt or woolen sash, and old men frequently wore another sash decorated with tassels dangling at the side. Men also wore a breechclout, leggings, and moccasins. Headgear consisted of a cloth turban decorated with feathers (Speck 1909:46).

Women wore calico dresses, often ornamented with silver brooches and a beaded belt. Short leggings and moccasins were also worn, along with necklaces, earrings, and bracelets. On ceremonial occasions, they wore a large, curved, ornate comb from which ribbons of various colors streamed to the ground (Speck, *op. cit.*).

Hawkins (1848:62) says that the Yuchi were "more civil and orderly" than their neighbors, the Creeks. He regarded them as industrious and noted that they retained their own customs, even though they were then living among the Creeks. He further noted that "the men take part of the labors of the women, and are more constant in their attachment to their women than is usual among red people" (*ibid.*).

Yuchi political affairs were conducted by the Chief society or the Warrior society. These were male organizations, and every male belonged to one or the other by birth. The Chief society functioned in managing governmental affairs of the town, and was the equivalent of the White, or Peace organization of the Creeks. The Warrior society, on the other hand, advocated warfare and provided a war leader. Both societies had ceremonial functions.

Ceremonies generally took place during the full moon, and the ceremonial year began in mid- or late summer when the first corn ripened (Speck *op. cit.*:112). On the second day of this Green Corn ceremony, a New Fire ritual was performed and afterwards the men partook of the sacred Black Drink. The ceremonial ended with a feast and a ball game (*op. cit.*:115).

Like other southeastern tribes, the Yuchi society revolved around a clan system. Speck (*op. cit.*:70) says the clan "is a group in which membership is reckoned through maternal descent. The members of each clan believe that they are the relatives and, in some vague way, the descendants of certain pre-existing animals whose names and identity they now bear." The Yuchi had some twenty clans, of which the Bear, Wolf, Tortoise, and Deer clans were the most important. It was from these clans that town chiefs, priests, and ceremonial leaders were chosen.

The Yuchi economy was based on agriculture, hunting, fishing, and gathering. Speck (*op. cit.*:45) points out that "almost any kind of bird, animal, or fish that was large enough to bother with was used as food." The blowgun and bow and arrow were the primary hunting implements, but game was also taken by a variety of traps and snares.

As indicated above, the Yuchi moved about during the early historic period. While some ultimately were incorporated by their old enemies, the Cherokees (Swanton 1922:298), most of the Yuchi allied themselves with the Creeks and lived among them. It was these who maintained their identity as a separate tribal group. They were removed to Indian Territory along with the Creeks in the 1830's. Some Yuchi have returned to Georgia to visit the sites of their old towns. One visitor graciously donated many of his possessions to the Columbus Museum of Art and Science, where they are currently on display.

OTHER TRIBES

Among other tribes living in Georgia in historic times was a band of the Shawnee. Although their main settlements were along the Cumberland River in Tennessee and Kentucky, a band of Shawnee settled near what is now Augusta and in 1681 evicted the Westo Indians from the area (Swanton 1922:317). By 1708, the Shawnee had three towns on the Savannah River. Following the ill-fated Yamassee War, these groups began to split up. Some removed to the Chattahoochee in the vicinity of what is now Fort Gaines, while others moved to Pennsylvania to join other Indian groups there. The Shawnee who lived on the Chattahoochee continued to abide with the Creeks for some time. Swanton (*op. cit.*:320) indicates that they may have left the Creek country prior to the Removal but that friendship between the Creeks and Shawnees continued after the Removal.

Another group once living in Georgia was a band of Chickasaw Indians. The Chickasaw territory was in western Tennessee, but in 1737 a group is known to have moved from South Carolina to the vicinity of the newly established trading post at Augusta (Swanton *op. cit.*:418). They apparently continued living in the vicinity of Augusta until the American Revolution, afterwards going back to the main Chickasaw settlements (*op. cit.*:419).

Today, many Georgians are proud to trace their ancestry to some of Georgia's original inhabitants. Although most of the Indian people were forcibly evicted from Georgia during the Removal, scattered bands either evaded the troops or were hidden by sympathetic whites. One such band of Cherokees was living in Banks County as late as 1895, moving to Indian lands in North Carolina in that year (see White 1973). Other Indians had intermarried with whites and remained. Their descendants, proud of the Cherokee or Creek ancestry, number among some of Georgia's most prominent citizens, and are in many professions. May all of Georgia's citizens come to a greater appreciation of our state's Indian heritage.

REFERENCES: CHAPTER VII

Bartram, William, *Travels of William Bartram,* ed. by Mark Van Doren, Dover Publications, New 1955 York.

_____, "Observations on the Creek and Cherokee Indians," *Transactions* 1976 *of the American Ethnological Society,* Vol. III, Pt. I, Kraus Reprint Co., Millwood, New York (reprint of the 1853 edition).

Bourne, Edward Gaylord, ed., *Narratives of the Career of Hernando de Soto,* Vol. I, AMS Press, 1973 Inc., New York (reprint of the 1922 edition).

Corkran, David H., "A Small Postscript on the ways and manners of the Indians called Cherokees, 1969 the contents of the whole so that you may find everything in the pages," *Southern Indian Studies,* Vol. 21 (edited copy of Alexander Longe's manuscript of 1725).

Crane, Verner W., *The Southern Frontier 1670-1732,* Duke University Press, Durham, N.C. 1928

Gearing, Fred, *Priests and Warriors: Social Structure for Cherokee Politics in the 18th Century,* 1962 American Anthropological Association, Vol. 64, No. 5, Pt. 2, Memoir 93.

Gilbert, William H., Jr., *The Eastern Cherokees,* Bureau of American Ethnology, Bulletin 133, 1943 Anthropological Papers No. 23, Government Printing Office, Washington.

Hawkins, Benjamin, *A Sketch of the Creek Country in 1798 and 1799,* Georgia Historical Society 1848 Collections, Vol. 3, Pt. I.

_____, *Letters of Benjamin Hawkins, 1796-1806,* Georgia Historical 1916 Society Collections, Vol. 9.

Hudson, Charles, *The Southeastern Indians,* University of Tennessee Press, Knoxville. 1976

Jones, Charles C., Jr., *Antiquities of the Southern Indians, Particularly of the Georgia Tribes,* 1873 D. Appleton and Co., New York.

Lewis, Thomas M.N., and Madeline Kneberg, *Tribes That Slumber,* University of Tennessee Press, 1958 Knoxville.

Malone, Henry T., *Cherokees of the Old South*, University of Georgia Press, Athens.
1956

Mooney, James, "Myths of the Cherokees," *Bureau of American Ethnology, 19th Annual Report*,
1900   *Pt. 1, 1897-98*, Government Printing Office, Washington.

Speck, Frank G., *Ethnology of the Yuchi Indians*, Anthropological Publications of the University
1909   Museum, Vol. 1, No. 1, University of Pennsylvania, Philadelphia.

Spencer, Robert F., Jesse D. Jennings, et al., *The Native Americans*, 2nd Edition, Harper and Row,
1977   New York.

Swanton, John R., *Early History of the Creek Indians and Their Neighbors*, Bureau of American
1922   Ethnology, Bulletin 73, Government Printing Office, Washington.

_____, "Social Organization and Social Usages of the Indians of the Creek
1928a Confederacy," *Bureau of American Ethnology, 42nd Annual Report, 1924-25*, Government
     Printing Office, Washington.

_____, "Religious Beliefs and Medical Practices of the Creek Indians,"
1928   *Bureau of American Ethnology, 42nd Annual Report, 1924-25*, Government Printing Office,
     Washington.

_____, *The Indians of the Southeastern United States*, Bureau of Ameri-
1946   can Ethnology, Bulletin 137, Government Printing Office, Washington.

White, Max E., "Cherokee Indians in Northeast Georgia After the Removal," Paper presented at
1973   the Southern Anthropological Society meeting, Wrightsville Beach, N.C.

_____, "An Ethnoarchaeological Approach to Cherokee Subsistence and
1980   Settlement Patterns," unpublished Ph.D. dissertation, Indiana University, Bloomington,
     Indiana.

Williams, Samuel Cole, ed., *Adair's History of the American Indians*, The Watauga Press, Johnson
1930   City, Tennessee.

_____, ed., *Lieut. Henry Timberlake's Memoirs, 1756-1765*, Continental
1948   Book Co., Marietta, Georgia.